THE
BIBLE'S BIG STORY
IN THE OLD TESTAMENT

CASKET EMPTY STUDENT EDITION

The Casket Empty Bible Series

Casket Empty Old Testament Bible Study

Casket Empty New Testament Bible Study

Casket Empty Old Testament Study Guide

Casket Empty New Testament Study Guide

Casket Empty Old Testament Timeline

Casket Empty New Testament Timeline

Casket Empty Old Testament Maps

Casket Empty New Testament Maps

Casket Empty Old Testament PowerPoints

Casket Empty New Testament PowerPoints

www.casketempty.com

CASKET EMPTY BIBLE SERIES

THE BIBLE'S BIG STORY IN THE OLD TESTAMENT

CASKET EMPTY STUDENT EDITION

CHELSEA KINGSTON ERICKSON

CAROL M. KAMINKSI, SERIES EDITOR

Casket Empty Media LLC.
www.casketempty.com

Casket Empty Media LLC.
www.casketempty.com

ISBN: 979-8-9915611-1-2

Interior design by Creative Publishing Book Design.
Cover design and icons by Nicole Rim.

Contents

Dear Reader,

Welcome to an exciting new journey in understanding God's Word, the Bible. I'm so glad you're here.

As we begin, I can't help but think about the exchange between Bilbo Baggins and the great wizard Gandalf in J.R.R. Tolkien's *The Hobbit.* Approaching Bilbo's cozy home in the Shire, Gandalf declares, "I am looking for someone to share in an adventure I am arranging..."

After the hobbit outlines all the reasons he does not wish to participate in any such adventure, Gandalf promises Bilbo that he'll have a tale to tell when he returns. Tentatively, Bilbo asks, "You can promise that I'll come back?"

Gandalf replies: "No. And if you do, you will not be the same."

I can assure you that this adventure of discovering the Bible's story is not quite so dangerous as the one Gandalf had in mind! Still, I am certain that after studying God's Word for yourself, *you will not be the same.*

Whether you are brand new to studying the Bible, or you've been learning about Scripture your whole life, God's Word is powerful to shape your life and change you in the most wonderful ways.

The Bible Is One Story

The Bible is the true story that God uses to reveal himself to human beings. We read the Bible, God's own Word to us, *so that we can know who God is and grow in relationship with him.* In this study you'll discover that the Bible is one story in two parts: the Old Testament and New Testament.

The Bible tells us about God's desire to be in relationship with us. Things take a turn for the worse at the beginning of the story, but God has a plan to rescue us from sin (our rebellion against him) and to redeem us for relationship with him. God fulfills this plan through the life, death, and resurrection of his Son, Jesus, who forgives sinners and calls us into his family. That's really good news!

And the even better news is that the Bible's story isn't finished. God promises that one day, Jesus will come again to restore the whole world so that it brings him glory. Jesus will reign forever as king, and God's people—those from every nation and language who have trusted in Jesus—will live with him forever. This story includes all those who put their trust in Jesus.

Casket Empty Student Edition

You'll be learning about the words Casket Empty shortly, but the *Student Edition* of Casket Empty you hold in your hands will lead you through the Old Testament in 18 weeks—hopefully alongside a group of friends and some adults who love you and want to help you grow in Jesus. You can continue your study of the Bible by doing the Casket Empty New Testament study, which will take you through the entire New Testament in 14 weeks. These Old and New Testament *Student Edition* studies match the Old and New Testament Casket Empty Bible Studies in the same series written for adults. If your whole church is doing a Casket Empty Bible Study, you'll be able to compare notes with your parents or other adults about what you're learning since you'll be covering the same Bible passages each week.

The *Student Edition* of Casket Empty has been written specifically for you. The questions are written with high schoolers in mind, but they can be adapted to fit a middle school or even a young adult audience. You can use the *Student Edition* studies in your youth group, Sunday school, small group, Bible class, homeschool co-op, or even one-on-one with a parent or youth leader. I recommend that you take turns reading the Bible passages and summaries out loud together. Then include as much participation as time will allow.

In each week's discussion questions, you'll become familiar with the categories of *observe*, *interpret*, and *apply*. Praying for God's Spirit to instruct us, we first make *observations* about the passage and reflect on its details. Then we move to *interpretation* based on our initial observations. Finally, we consider how we might *apply* the passage to our own lives, asking God for help to grow in his grace. As part of this final step, each week we make *connections* between the Old and New Testaments to guide our understanding of God's Word. Our goal is that you will gain confidence in understanding the Bible's big story. If you are an adult leading this study, a Parent and Leader's Guide is available on the Casket Empty website (www.casketempty.com) that explains how to lead the study, and it includes teaching tips designed specifically for youth.

Knowing Jesus Through the Old Testament

Knowing God as he reveals himself in his Word is the boldest, most wonderful adventure you could ever undertake! As you complete this journey through the Old Testament, the creators of Casket Empty and I are praying that you will come to know the story's Hero—Jesus, who lived the perfect life, died in place of sinners, and rose again to conquer sin and death forever. As you encounter him, I trust that you will never be the same.

In Jesus,

Chelsea Erickson

WEEK 1

One Redemptive Story

The Bible is one redemptive story that points to Jesus.

Icebreaker Questions

Say your name and tell the group about a story you love—whether it's a book, a movie, or a series.

In your opinion, what makes a really good story? What are some elements that draw you in and make you want to keep reading?

Today we're going to begin journeying through God's story, the Bible, together. We're going to see that many of these elements of good storytelling are part of the best story ever told.

What's the Bible All About?

Depending on your familiarity with the Bible, you may know that it is full of stories about God's people. You may also know that it contains God's instructions for how his people are to live. But did you know that the Bible is one continuous story, from the first book of Genesis to the final book of Revelation? All the smaller stories in the Bible fit together to tell the *one story* of redemption—God rescues people for relationship with himself.

The Bible tells the story of redemption in two parts: the Old Testament and the New Testament. You may have heard people say that the God of the Old Testament is somehow different from the God of the New Testament, but that is not what the Bible itself teaches. Throughout the Old and New Testaments, God reveals that his character is steadfast and unchanging. Over the weeks of our study, we will learn that God is "the compassionate and gracious God, slow to anger, abounding in love and faithfulness, maintaining love to thousands, and forgiving wickedness, rebellion and sin. Yet he does not leave the guilty unpunished..." (Exod. 34:6–7).

The Old Testament begins the story with God's good creation. God creates human beings for relationship with himself, but Adam and Eve go their own way, rebelling against their Creator. The Bible calls this rebellion *sin,* and it affects every human heart, damaging the good world God has made. But the rest of the Bible reveals God's plan to restore people to relationship with himself. We have a long story ahead of us, yet at the close of the Old Testament, we are still waiting for the fulfillment of God's promises. God will send his promised king (known as the "Messiah") to save his people.

The New Testament tells the story of the Messiah's coming. His name is Jesus, God's own Son, who saves his people from their sin. The words Casket Empty capture the message of the whole Bible. The first man God creates and names Adam, brings about death for humanity when he sins, but God sends his own Son to conquer the grave. Jesus dies on a cross and then rises from the dead, putting an end to sin and death forever. God invites us to join him in this pattern of life. When we trust Jesus in faith, our lives are united with his. We die to sin and rise with him, and we will live with God forever, with Jesus as our King! Jesus gives us the Holy Spirit to live within us now so that we can join his mission in the world until he returns to fully restore creation.

 The Bible's Big Story Through Casket Empty

In our study this week, we'll learn that *the Bible is one redemptive story that points to Jesus.* This study is structured around the acronym Casket Empty, which will help you learn the Bible's big story. The Old Testament is traced through six key periods (Casket), and the New Testament is traced through five key periods (Empty). The phrase Casket Empty will help you remember that Jesus' death and resurrection are at the center of the biblical story. Let's work on memorizing this acronym together to help us understand the main plot of the Bible. Here's a summary of all the letters in Casket Empty:

C = Creation	**E** = Expectations
A = Abraham	**M** = Messiah
S = Sinai	**P** = Pentecost
K = Kings	**T** = Teaching
E = Exile	**Y** = Yet-to-come
T = Temple	

An *Old Testament* Casket Empty *Timeline* is also available in this series, and you may want to have your own copy so that you can trace the story of the Old Testament visually using the timeline. If you want to dive deeper into the Old Testament, additional readings from the Casket Empty *Old Testament Study Guide* are provided at the end of each lesson. In this study we will be using the acronym Casket for the Old Testament portion of our study. Each period of the acronym Casket is represented by a picture that will help you remember six key events in the Old Testament, which is the first part of the Bible's big story. I would encourage you to memorize the pictures along with each letter, as we'll be using them throughout this study.

Creation: The picture of two trees represents the creation story and the two trees God places in the Garden of Eden.

Abraham: The picture of a gift represents God's grace shown to Abraham and the promises God makes.

Sinai: The picture of the Ten Commandments represents the giving of the law at Mount Sinai under Moses.

Kings: The picture of a crown represents the kings who reign over God's people in the land of Israel.

Exile: The picture of a bird of prey represents the curses of the covenant that come upon God's people when they go into exile to Babylon.

Temple: The picture of a temple represents the rebuilt temple after the period of exile when God restores his people.

Books of the Old Testament

The Old Testament contains thirty-nine books covering three types of literature: books about Israel's history (Genesis to Esther; the first five books are known as the Torah), poetical books (Job to Song of Solomon), and prophetical books (Isaiah to Malachi).

The challenge for us as we read the Old Testament is that not all the books are in chronological order. This can make it tricky to know where you are in the storyline. Our study of the Old Testament through Casket Empty will help you trace the storyline of the Old Testament so that you can better understand the Bible's "big story." Jesus taught his disciples that the Old Testament pointed to him. This week we will look at his conversation with two of his followers just after he had risen from the dead. We're going to discover that the ***Bible is one redemptive story that points to Jesus.***

Bible Readings

Matthew 1:1; Luke 24:13-35; 1 Corinthians 15:1–4

Observe

Read Luke 24:13–35. Share the who, what, when, and where of this passage.

What did Jesus say to his disciples about himself in this passage (vv. 25–27, see also vv. 44–47)?

Read 1 Corinthians 15:1–4. When the writers of the New Testament refer to the Scriptures, they are referring to the Old Testament specifically. In these verses, what events about Jesus are foretold in the Scriptures according to Paul?

Interpret

Does it surprise you that Jesus says the Old Testament points to himself? Why or why not?

How does Paul agree with Jesus on this point in his letter to the Corinthian church?

If you are familiar with the Bible, can you think of any Old Testament passages that point ahead to the death and/or resurrection of Jesus?

Apply

How do the words about Jesus in these verses inform the way we should read the Old Testament?

Connecting the Bible's Big Story

Read Matthew 1:1. How does this verse help us understand the big story we see unfolding throughout the Bible? As you discuss, remember that "Christ" is not a last name. Instead, it means "anointed one," just like the English word "Messiah."

What are some questions you have about the Old Testament as we begin this study together?

Gospel Application

Jesus makes it clear in his conversation on the road to Emmaus that the whole Bible is about him. As the Son of God, he is the one to whom the prophets pointed and the one who makes the Father known. All of God's glorious character—his loyalty to his people, his faithfulness to his promises, his justice, mercy, and goodness—are on full display in Jesus Christ.

Similarly, in 1 Corinthians 15, Paul describes the *gospel*, that is, the message of the good news about Jesus. Paul tells the Corinthians that the Old Testament specifically taught that God's promised Messiah would die, be buried, and then rise again. Jesus' fulfillment of these promises shows that he really is from God. Jesus is God's beloved Son. This is truly *good news* because it means that Jesus has the power to save.

The authors of the New Testament understood that they were building upon the foundation of the Old Testament as they told the story of God's work through his Son, Jesus. For example, Matthew describes Jesus as "the Messiah, the son of David, the son of Abraham," linking Jesus directly to two Old Testament figures who received God's promises (Matt. 1:1).

You may still have a lot of questions about the Old Testament. Over the coming weeks of our study, we'll have an opportunity to read through several passages from each section of the Old Testament timeline together. We'll grow together in our understanding of God's work to rescue his people. For now, it's most important to know that God has revealed his redemptive plan to us so that we can know him *personally*. If that's a new idea for you, please talk with a youth leader or parent who follows Jesus—these adults would love to tell you more.

Additional Bible Readings

John 1:1–14; 2 Timothy 3:14–17

Dig Deeper with the *Old Testament Study Guide*

Read the introduction (pp. xi-xvii)

Bible Study Notes

WEEK 2

God's Good Creation

God creates a good world and fills it with his royal representatives.

Icebreaker Questions

Say your name and share whether you prefer the mountains or the beach.

Which of these is your favorite place to spend time outdoors, and why?

In our lesson this week we'll see how God reveals himself as the Creator, forming the earth and everything in it by his powerful word.

The Bible's Big Story

- Can anyone remember what the letters in the CASKET acronym stand for?
- We're currently in the part of the biblical story we refer to as CREATION because God creates the world and everything in it.
- The picture for the period of CREATION is two trees representing the creation story.

- Last week we learned that *the Bible is one redemptive story that points to Jesus.*
- This week we're going to discover that ***God creates a good world and fills it with his royal representatives.***

Setting the Stage

The Bible begins with these words: "In the beginning God created the heavens and the earth" (Gen. 1:1). The first chapter of the Bible opens with the dawn of creation, recording God's stunning artistry in forming the heavens and the earth. In order for us to appreciate the Bible's account, we need to remember that when Moses wrote Genesis, the world was largely *polytheistic*. People believed in many gods. By contrast, the Bible insists there is only *one God.* His name is Yahweh, which our English Bible usually translates as "Lord" (as in Gen. 2:4).

In Genesis 1:2 we read that "the earth was formless and empty, darkness was over the surface of the deep," but God's Spirit hovered over the darkness. God now begins to order and fill the earth. On each of the seven days in this chapter, we read: "And God said," emphasizing that God alone has authority to create and he does this through his Word. The number seven signifies wholeness or perfection, emphasizing the completeness of God's work. At the conclusion of each day, we read that "God saw that it was good."

Some scholars see the days of creation as 24-hour periods. Others interpret each day as a longer time, and they have noticed that day one corresponds with day four, day two corresponds with day five, and day three corresponds with day six. You'll see this view (known as the "framework view") represented in the chart below.

Day 1 – Light	Day 4 – Sun, Moon, Stars
Day 2 – Sky, Separating Waters	Day 5 – Birds, Fish
Day 3 – Dry Land, Vegetation	Day 6 – Creatures, Humans
Day 7 Sabbath	

Churches have different views on the creation week, but the two views I've mentioned affirm that God is the Creator. He created the world and all living creatures, including human beings.

On day six, God not only finishes creating the animal kingdom, but the creation story slows down as God creates human beings in his image. Human beings are different from the animals as his unique image-bearers, and this means that God makes people for relationship with himself. Together, human beings, both male and female, will fulfill the responsibility of ruling God's world. As part of this design, God intends for marriage to take place between one man and one woman.

Bible Readings

Genesis 1:24–2:3; 2:15–25; John 1:1–5; Colossians 1:15–18

Observe

Read Genesis 1:24–2:3. Describe what we see God creating in these verses. What do you see repeated?

How does God evaluate his creation on this sixth and final day of his creative work? Compare this to what he has said at the end of each day prior to this point in the narrative.

How does God provide for the human beings he has made?

Read Genesis 2:15–25. What additional command does the Lord give the man in Genesis 2?

What new information do we learn in Genesis 2 about the relationship between the first man and woman?

 Interpret

What are the specific tasks God has called human beings to carry out? See if you can come up with a list from both passages. You may want to do this in pairs and report back to the group.

What do these two passages teach about what it means to be created in God's image and after his likeness (Gen. 1:26–28)?

What do you think the author wants to convey by pointing out that God rested from his work on day seven?

 Apply

In the ancient world with its belief in many gods, the opening chapters of Genesis were revolutionary. What do these passages teach us about the origins of human life that might be different from what you have heard at school or elsewhere?

How do God's words of blessing and commission in Genesis 1:28 give direction to our lives?

 Connecting the Bible's Big Story

Read John 1:1–5. What do these verses tell us about Jesus' role in creating the world with the Father?

If time permits, read Colossians 1:15–18 together.

How do these verses help us understand the big story we see unfolding throughout the Bible?

 Gospel Application

In these opening chapters of the Bible's story, we see how God creates the world and calls everything he has made "very good." He forms human beings in his own image to rule and to care for the world as his representatives. Other ancient texts tell us that statues or idols often represented specific gods in a temple. In ancient rituals, priests would breathe into an idol's nostrils to signify the presence of the deity. But in the biblical narrative, the one true God forms *living beings* to be in relationship with him. God animates them with his own breath, and he gives them a purpose and mission in the world.

Understanding this ancient context helps us understand that Adam and Eve have a priestly role in the garden. They have been created to worship God and to bring him glory. As we read through the Old Testament together over the next few weeks, we'll see that some of the language about Eden is used to describe the tabernacle and the temple—places God will designate to meet personally with his people.

Sadly, in next week's readings we will find that Adam and Eve—and all human beings after them—will rebel against their Creator. This is why Jesus came into the world and lived among us: he is the perfect image of God that we all have failed to be. He rescues us and draws us back into God's family.

If you've ever wondered about your purpose in the world, the opening chapters of Genesis are a good place to start. God has created you in his own image for relationship with him. He invites you to contribute to the flourishing of his world. And if you've ever wondered what God is really like, then look to Jesus, who is "the image of the invisible God" and "in him all things were created" (Col. 1:15–16). Like Adam and Eve, you were made to worship God and to help others see his goodness.

Additional Bible Readings

Psalm 8

Review Old Testament Timeline

Review the Creation section on the timeline.

Dig Deeper with the *Old Testament Study Guide*

Read the first section of chapter one: Creation (pp. 1-14).

Bible Study Notes

WEEK 3

Relationships Ruptured

Adam and Eve sin in the garden and relationships are ruptured.

Icebreaker Questions

Say your name and share about something or someone in your life that reveals the goodness of God's creation.

What do you notice in the world around you that shows things are not as they should be?

Today we'll read about how the first human beings rebel against God, revealing the central problem of the Bible's story.

The Bible's Big Story

- Let's review the letters in the CASKET acronym.
- We're currently in the part of the biblical story we refer to as CREATION because God creates the world and everything in it.
- Last week we learned that *God creates a good world and fills it with his royal representatives.*

- This week we're going to discover that ***Adam and Eve sin in the garden and relationships are ruptured.***

 Setting the Stage

How often have you read a book or watched a movie that starts out with a happy scene, and then quickly turns into conflict and struggle? The Bible's narrative begins with a beautiful scene to set the stage. Then the author of Genesis describes a serious problem in need of resolution.

We closed our Bible reading together last week observing *good relationships*—between God and people, between Adam and Eve, and between people and God's creation. But our opening passage today immediately takes a sinister turn as we meet the villain of the story: "Now the serpent was more crafty than any of the wild animals the LORD God had made" (Gen. 3:1). This wicked serpent will oppose God's good plan for his creation.

The Lord has already told Adam that he and Eve are free to eat anything they would like in God's beautiful garden—*except* for the fruit that comes from the tree of the knowledge of good and evil (Gen. 2:15–17). Because they are his royal representatives, God calls Adam and Eve to trust in him and to obey this one command. But as we'll read in a moment, a wicked serpent will call this command into question, using subtle (but damaging) lies to entice Adam and Eve away from obeying the voice of God.

Adam and Eve will choose their own way instead of God's, and they disobey his command. The Bible calls this *sin*, and it brings death and destruction into the good world God has made. Worst of all, it damages all the good relationships—between people and God, between people, and even between people and creation. Where there once was harmony in God's good creation, now there will be struggle, suffering, and pain.

Bible Readings

Genesis 3:1–24; 6:5–22; Matthew 4:1–11; Romans 5:12–21

Observe

Read Genesis 3:1–24. Summarize the who, what, when, and where of this passage.

Describe the conversation between God and his people. What did God say to Adam, and what was his response? What did Eve say when God addressed her?

How is God's judgment seen in the story, first against the serpent, and then Adam and Eve for their sin? What did God do for Adam and Eve in spite of their rebellion?

Read Genesis 6:5–22. How does the author of Genesis describe the extent of human sin after the time of Adam and Eve (Gen. 6:5–7, 11–13)? What words does the author use to emphasize the seriousness of the situation?

How does the author describe Noah in contrast to the rest of his generation (Gen. 6:8–10, 22)?

 Interpret

Did the serpent accurately reflect God's commands to Adam in the questions he asked Eve? (Take a look at Gen. 2:15–17 to compare.)

In Genesis 2, God had told Adam that if he ate from the tree of the knowledge of good and evil, he would surely die. We know that Adam does die (Gen. 5:5), but what else happens to Adam and Eve that suggests a spiritual death away from God's presence?

Based on what you have read in Genesis 3 and 6, do you think the serpent succeeds in his plan to lure human beings away from God's rule? Why or why not? Do you see any evidence that God will continue to carry out his good plans for the world?

 Apply

After Adam and Eve have sinned, they hear God coming and hide from him. Can you recall a time when you tried to hide your sin—or even yourself—from God or others? (Share if you feel comfortable.) Why do you think our human impulse is to hide our sin?

In Genesis 6, we see the principle at work that sin leads to death (Gen. 2:15–17). But God extends grace to Noah and his family. What does this show us about God's character?

When you know that you have disobeyed God, how could it help you to remember God's grace to Adam, Eve, and Noah's family?

 Connecting the Bible's Big Story

Read Matthew 4:1–11. How is Jesus victorious in obeying God, whereas Adam and Eve (and every human being since) fail to obey?

Read Romans 5:12–15. (If time permits, read Romans 5:12–21.) How do these verses help us understand the big story we see unfolding throughout the Bible?

 Gospel Application

Genesis 3 establishes the problem of human sin in the midst of God's good world. God commissions Adam and Eve to represent him in the world he has made, but they try to find life apart from God. As a result, Adam and Eve, and all human beings after them, experience the effects of what Christians call *the fall* (our separation from God and from each other). We even experience separation from creation as our work so often feels like pointless toil. Now God's good creation is tarnished by sin, and human beings are powerless to undo the awful result.

By the time of Noah, the world has become so corrupt that God decides to blot out human beings, but mercifully, God shows grace to Noah (Gen. 6:8). We read further in Genesis 9:13–17 that God promises never again to destroy his creation by a flood. But human sin continues, and along with it comes the pain of separation from God.

The whole Bible from Genesis to Revelation is the story of God's good plan to redeem the world he created, restoring human beings to himself and bringing restoration to his creation. God has sent his own Son into the world to redeem what Adam's sin has torn apart. The apostle Paul writes: "For if the many died by the trespass of the one man, how much more did God's grace and the gift that came by the grace of the one man, Jesus Christ, overflow to the many!" (Rom. 5:15).

Because Jesus is both fully God and fully human, he is the only person who can ever restore what was broken in the garden. Adam and Eve fail in their mission to stand up to the serpent, but Jesus has defeated him on the cross!

When you find yourself confronted by the brokenness of the world and the sin in your own heart, look to Jesus. He is the perfectly obedient Son of God who has defeated Satan on your behalf. In Jesus, God is redeeming all those who trust in him. And one day, he will restore the whole created world as well.

Additional Bible Readings

Genesis 4; 1 Corinthians 15:20–49

Review Old Testament Timeline

Review the Creation section on the timeline.

Dig Deeper with the *Old Testament Study Guide*

Read the second section of chapter one: Creation (pp. 14-25).

Bible Study Notes

WEEK 4

God’s Faith Family

God makes promises to Abraham and Sarah and establishes his faith family.

 Icebreaker Questions

Say your name and tell the group about a gift you’ve received that stands out in your memory.

When we’re little, waiting for a Christmas or birthday gift might seem like waiting forever. What are some things we wait for as we grow older? Is it ever hard for you to wait to see God fulfill his promises?

In today’s passage, we’ll learn how God keeps his promises to a man named Abraham, and how we can know God will continue to do what he has promised.

 The Bible’s Big Story

- Let’s review the letters in the CASKET acronym.

- We're currently in the part of the biblical story we refer to as Abraham because God chooses a man called Abraham and promises to bless his family.
- The picture for the period of Abraham is a gift representing God's grace.
- Last week we learned that *Adam and Eve sin in the garden and relationships are ruptured.*
- This week we're going to discover that ***God makes promises to Abraham and Sarah and establishes his faith family.***

Setting the Stage

Today's readings mark a major turning point in the Bible's storyline. Many generations after Noah and the flood, God chooses a man named Abram and his wife Sarai to begin a family that will represent him in the world. God eventually changes their names to Abraham and Sarah as a sign of all he will do through them. When the Lord first speaks to Abraham, he says, "Go from your country, your people and your father's household to the land I will show you" (Gen. 12:1). In Abraham's day, these instructions were unusual, as most people lived near their families.

It's important for us to realize that Abraham doesn't know the one true God when he receives this radical call from the Lord. He and his family live in an ancient city called Ur, which is known for worshiping a pagan moon god called Sin. People in the ancient world worshiped idols, seeking to secure blessings from the gods in areas such as fertility, agriculture, and warfare. The book of Joshua later tells us that Abraham's family worshiped idols (Josh. 24:2).

Despite their idolatrous background, God chooses Abraham and Sarah, calling them by his grace to play a special role in his redemptive plan. God gives Abram several promises: God will bring Abraham into a new land and make him a great nation. He will bless Abraham and make his name great, and all the families of the earth will be blessed through his descendants (Gen. 12:1–3). But these promises won't happen right away, as we'll read in Genesis 15.

Bible Readings

Genesis 12:1–3; 15:1–21; 22:1–24;
Romans 4:18–25; Galatians 3:6–29

Observe

Read Genesis 12:1–3 and 15:1–21. God makes promises to Abraham in Genesis 12:1-3. A few years later, which of God's promises does Abraham seem to have trouble believing, and why?

What does the Lord say to Abraham to reassure him? How does Abraham respond to God's reassurance (15:8)?

What does God ask Abraham to do?

Read Genesis 22:1–24. When we read the story in Genesis 22, we learn that God has given Abraham and Sarah the son he has promised them. What does God command Abraham to do in the beginning verses of this chapter?

How does Abraham respond? Share specific details from the passage.

What does the angel of the Lord do in the story so that Abraham does not need to offer up his son? Summarize the angel of the Lord's words in verses 15–18.

 Interpret

The word "righteousness" means *right-standing with God.* What do you think it means that Abraham "believed the LORD, and he credited it to him as righteousness" (Gen. 15:6)?

In God's covenant relationship with Abraham, what does God pledge to do, and what does he require from Abraham? How might this relationship differ from the way people worshiped pagan gods in Abraham's day?

What do we learn from Genesis 15 and 22 about God's character? What do we learn about his commitment to his people?

 Apply

Do you think there is anything in your life that God might ask you to be willing to set aside or offer up in obedience to him? Where do you need his help in order to trust him with these things?

 Connecting the Bible's Big Story

Read Romans 4:18–25. How does Paul explain what it means that Abraham's faith was "credited to him as righteousness?" What does God do for us when we put our faith in Jesus (vv. 23–25)?

Read Galatians 3:10–14 (Or if time permits, read Gal. 3:6–29). How do these verses help us understand the big story we see unfolding throughout the Bible?

 Gospel Application

Abraham and Sarah struggle to wait for God to fulfill his promises. They are required to wait many long years for the son and family God has pledged to give them—and at times they take matters into their own hands (see Gen. 16 and 20). Still, we read that Abraham "believed the LORD, and he credited it to him as righteousness" (Gen. 15:6). And in faith Abraham willingly offers up his beloved son (Gen. 22). God remains faithful to Abraham and Sarah, giving them a son in their old age and eventually doing all that he has promised through their family line.

The ultimate fulfillment of God's promises to Abraham happens when God sends Jesus as a member of Abraham's family line, blessing all nations through the forgiveness he brings. The way God relates to Abraham in Genesis 15 and 22 points ahead to Jesus' saving work in two ways.

First, God's covenant with Abraham shows that he is fully committed to the people he calls to himself. God sends Jesus to die for our sin and establish a relationship with us. When we put our trust in Jesus, like Abraham, our faith is counted as righteousness so that we can be in right standing with God.

Second, God's provision of a ram for the sacrifice points forward to the way Jesus will die in our place, absorbing the penalty for our sin. When we struggle to believe God or trust in his promises, we can look to Jesus, who fulfills every single one.

Additional Bible Readings

Genesis 17:1–8; 18:1–14; Romans 4:1–25; 9:6–9

Review Old Testament Timeline and Maps

Review the ABRAHAM section on the timeline and familiarize yourself with the Abrahamic promises listed.

Review the first map, *Abraham's Journey to the Promised Land.* Trace Abraham's journey from Ur to Canaan, identifying key cities along his path.

Dig Deeper with the *Old Testament Study Guide*

Read the first section of chapter two: Abraham (pp. 27-51).

Bible Study Notes

WEEK 5

Israel's Family Preserved

Israel's family is preserved as God continues to show his faithfulness.

Icebreaker Questions

Say your name and briefly share your favorite family tradition or memory.

What are some things that can also make family life difficult? Why do you think family relationships can be so challenging, even when we love one another?

Today's readings show us how God is faithful to the faith family he creates, even in the midst of relational difficulties.

The Bible's Big Story

- Let's review the letters in the CASKET acronym.
- We're currently in the part of the biblical story we refer to as ABRAHAM because God chooses a man called Abraham and promises to bless his family.

- Last week we learned that *God makes promises to Abraham and Sarah and establishes his faith family.*
- This week we're going to discover that ***Israel's family is preserved as God continues to show his faithfulness.***

 Setting the Stage

Our readings for today include a heavy dose of family drama. From sibling rivalry, to parents showing favoritism, to lies and deception—the family God has chosen struggles with ongoing dysfunction. And still, God shows his faithfulness to them.

Abraham's son Isaac and his wife, Rebekah, have twin boys named Jacob and Esau. Because Esau is the oldest, he is supposed to receive the largest portion of his father's inheritance. But God had told Rebekah that her older son would serve the younger son (Gen. 25:23). When Isaac is old, Rebekah and Jacob work together to trick Isaac into giving Esau's firstborn blessing to Jacob.

But when Esau hears what has happened, he plots to kill his brother, so Isaac and Rebekah send Jacob north to a place called Haran, where his uncle lives. Rebekah hopes her brother Laban will find Jacob a wife.

Along his journey when Jacob stops to sleep one night, God makes promises to him in a dream that reaffirm his covenantal promises to Abraham and to Isaac (cf. Gen. 12:1-3; 26:2-5). In yet another story of sibling rivalry, Jacob marries not just one, but *two* of Laban's daughters named Rachel and Leah. Although this might seem strange to us in view of God's creational design for marriage between a man and a woman, ancient people sometimes practiced polygamy (even though not God's design from the beginning).

Jacob has twelve sons through his wives, Rachel and Leah, and their two servants. Just as Jacob's mother played favorites, Jacob also loves his son Joseph more than the rest of his children. Joseph's brothers hate him because their father gives Joseph a special coat and because Joseph tells his brothers about a dream in which they bow down to him.

The brothers eventually throw Joseph into a pit and sell him as a slave, but God is with Joseph. He eventually becomes second in command to the pharaoh of Egypt, where God uses him to provide for Egypt and his own family during a seven-year famine. Eventually, Joseph's brothers come to Egypt seeking food, and the family is reunited.

Bible Readings

Genesis 28:10–22; 50:15–26;
Romans 9:1–16; Hebrews 11:20–22

Observe

Read Genesis 28:10–22. Summarize the who, what, when, and where of the passage.

List the different promises that God makes to Jacob.

What does Jacob vow to God?

Read Genesis 50:15–26. What do Joseph's brothers fear when they realize their father is dead?

What do the brothers tell Joseph in response to their fear? How does Joseph respond to the words of his brothers?

As Joseph is dying, what does he proclaim God will do for his descendants?

 Interpret

What are some of the difficult family dynamics in these passages?

How do we see God continuing to keep his promises to Abraham's family?

What do Joseph's words in chapter 50 tell us about his experience of God's care for him?

 Apply

All of us are sinful and flawed, just like the people we've read about in our study today. How have you experienced God's presence and provision in your life, even when you haven't been faithful to him?

 Connecting the Bible's Big Story

Read Hebrews 11:20–22. Even though there are many dramas in these families, God is building his faith family through them. How does Hebrews 11 point to the faith of Isaac, Jacob, and Joseph? (See also vv. 39–40.)

Read Romans 9:6–13. (If time permits, read vv. 1–16.) How do these verses help us understand the big story we see unfolding throughout the Bible?

 Gospel Application

The Bible is incredibly realistic about the pain we sometimes feel with those we love most. All of the families we've looked at in our study today sin against one another, even as God is working out his plans through them. We see his transformational work in each of their lives, as they come to know him personally—and he even works to restore their relationships with one another. Ultimately, God uses these complicated families as part of his plan to rescue people for himself.

Jacob's sons and two grandsons become the heads of the twelve tribes of Israel (Gen. 49:28). During the days of Joshua, the tribes will each be allocated a portion of the land God promised to Abraham's family. Jacob's son Judah and his family will play a special role in the history of Israel and in God's redemptive plan. All the kings of Israel's southern kingdom will come through Judah's line, beginning with King David. When God sends his own Son into the world to redeem it, he will also come from the line of Judah, which identifies him as a descendant of David.

Jesus is the true son of Abraham, and he will bring those who trust him into God's forever family (Rom. 9:6-8). We recognize our need for Jesus' rescue and redemption as we experience sin in our lives and in our families. If you are facing a painful situation in your family now, know that you are not alone. God sees and loves your family, just as he loved Isaac and Jacob's family. In his timing, he can work to restore your family relationships by his Spirit. In the meantime, he calls you to be a part of his "faith family" through the work of Jesus on your behalf.

Additional Bible Readings

Genesis 27; 35–50

Review Old Testament Timeline and Maps

Review the ABRAHAM section on the timeline.

Review the first map, *Abraham's Journey to the Promised Land.* Locate the region of Paddan Aram, the city of Shechem, and the land of Goshen in Egypt.

Dig Deeper with the *Old Testament Study Guide*

Read the last section of chapter two: Abraham (pp. 51-54).

Bible Study Notes

WEEK 6

God Rescues and Reveals

God rescues Israel from slavery and reveals himself as the one true God.

Icebreaker Questions

Say your name and briefly share about a time when you've experienced a "mountaintop high" of excitement (for example, a summer camp experience or spending time in nature).

Given a choice between head knowledge of something or a personal experience, which do you think most people would choose? Why?

Today's readings begin and end with personal encounters between God and his people.

The Bible's Big Story

- Let's review the letters in the CASKET acronym.
- We're currently in the part of the biblical story we refer to as SINAI because God is leading his people through the Sinai wilderness.

- The picture for the period of SINAI is the Ten Commandments representing God's law given to Moses.
- Last week we learned that *Israel's faith family is preserved as God continues to show his faithfulness.*
- This week we're going to discover that ***God rescues Israel from slavery and reveals himself as the one true God.***

 Setting the Stage

Following the death of Joseph, a new pharaoh of Egypt enslaves Joseph's descendants, which God had told Abraham would happen (Gen. 15:13). But God multiplies the generations of Abraham's family (Exod. 1:7; cf. Gen. 1:28), even as they labor building Pharaoh's cities.

Pharaoh feels threatened and commands the midwives to kill every Hebrew baby boy. But the midwives fear the Lord and let the boys live, including a Hebrew boy called Moses, who grows up in Pharaoh's household. As an adult, Moses kills an Egyptian slave master when he sees him mistreating a Hebrew slave. Moses then runs away to the wilderness, where he lives for 40 years.

One day, Moses encounters a bush that is burning, but strangely not burning up. God tells Moses to remove his sandals because he is standing on holy ground—a signal that a holy God is present.

God explains that he is aware of his people's suffering and that he will come down to deliver them from Egypt into the land he has promised. He instructs Moses to go to Pharaoh to bring his people out of Egypt. When Moses protests, God tells Moses his name: "I AM." God refers to himself by the Hebrew name Yahweh, which is a variation of his name, "I AM," since both are from the verb "to be" (*hayah*) in Hebrew. Our English Bibles often use "LORD" to convey this personal name for God. In our study, we refer to him as "Lord."

Pharaoh is hard of heart, and he will not listen to Moses and his brother Aaron. The Lord sends a series of plagues, demonstrating his ultimate power over Egypt and their gods, but Pharaoh will not relent. So, God finally announces that the firstborn son of every family in Egypt will die because Pharaoh has refused to let Israel (God's "firstborn son") go free. But God gives his people a way to be saved. By placing the blood of a spotless lamb over their doorframes, the Hebrews will be spared as the Angel of Death passes over their homes. God commands that his people observe the Passover every year as a reminder of his redemption.

Bible Readings

Exodus 14:10–31; 20:1–21; Acts 7:35–41;
Hebrews 9:15, 23–28

Observe

Read Exodus 14:10–31. This chapter describes the exodus from Egypt. What fears do the people express to Moses? How does Moses respond?

Turn to someone next to you and give a one sentence summary of how God delivers his people from slavery in Egypt. Then have several people share their summaries with the group.

Read Exodus 20:1–21. After the people arrive at Mount Sinai, how does God introduce himself to remind his people of what he has done for them?

What do the first four commandments share in common? What do the last six commandments share in common? What do all ten have in common?

What did the people see that made them fearful?

 Interpret

What similarities do you notice about the ways in which God shows his presence in these two chapters? (Exod. 14:19–20, 31; 20:18–21)

Why do you think the people respond as they do to the signs of God's presence with them in Exodus 20?

 Apply

How has God revealed himself to us in his Word? When is it hardest for you to believe who he says he is and to obey him?

 Connecting the Bible's Big Story

Read Acts 7:35–41. The New Testament believer Stephen spoke these words when he was on trial for his faith in Jesus. Why do you think it was important for him to include the story of Israel and God's covenant in his explanation of the gospel?

Read Hebrews 9:15, 23–28. How do these verses help us understand the big story we see unfolding throughout the Bible?

 Gospel Application

God gives Moses many other instructions in addition to the Ten Commandments. These include commands about loving God and loving one's neighbor. All these instructions show God's people what it means to be his holy people. Remember that God's relationship with his people is the central idea of his covenant.

In Exodus 20:2, God identifies himself as the Lord their God who brought them out of Egypt. Notice the order of things—first God tells Israel who he is and what he has done for them. *Then* he instructs them to obey his commands, which are for their flourishing. God's people are his "treasured possession." He has set them apart to be a "kingdom of priests and a holy nation" (Exod. 19:5–6), fulfilling his promise to Abraham to bless all the nations of the world through him.

When Moses shares God's law with the people, they cry out in one voice saying, "Everything the Lord has said we will do" (Exod. 24:3). We'll soon see how they struggle to keep these words.

Moses sprinkles the blood of animals on the people to confirm the covenant. The Lord's glory descends upon the mountain, and he calls Moses to come up to meet with him. The cloud of glory was a tangible sign of God's presence on Mount Sinai, giving assurance that he would fulfill his promise to dwell with his people and be their God.

God's revelation of himself—first to Moses in the burning bush, and then to all of Israel through the covenant on Mount Sinai—shows us that God is committed to being in relationship with his people. The writer to the Hebrews tells us that God has given us a new covenant in Christ that secures this relationship (Heb. 9:15). Jesus is the firstborn Son of God who sets us free from all the sins we have committed against God's law. Jesus died once and for all, rising from the dead, so that we can know God personally and have a relationship with him (Heb. 9:26–28).

Additional Bible Readings

Exodus 3:1–22; 24:1–18

Review Old Testament Timeline and Maps

Review the SINAI section on the timeline.

Review the second map, *The Exodus from Egypt.* Trace the journey of the Israelites from Egypt to the region of Mount Sinai.

Dig Deeper with the *Old Testament Study Guide*

Read the first part of chapter three: SINAI (pp. 55-69).

Bible Study Notes

God Dwells with His People

God makes a way to dwell with his people, even as they continue to sin against him.

Icebreaker Questions

Say your name and share about a place that is special to you.

What are some things that can make us feel attached to certain places?

Today we'll learn about the tabernacle—the special place where God will dwell with his people.

The Bible's Big Story

- Can anyone remember what the letters in the CASKET acronym stand for?
- We're currently in the part of the biblical story we refer to as SINAI because God is leading his people through the Sinai wilderness.

- Last week we learned that *God rescues Israel from slavery and reveals himself as the one true God.*
- This week we're going to discover that ***God makes a way to dwell with his people, even as they continue to sin against him.***

 Setting the Stage

Throughout the story of the Bible, we see that God is committed to being with his people—even though they continually sin against him. In Genesis 1, we learned that God created the world to be his holy dwelling place. But when Adam and Eve rebelled against God, he sent them out of the Garden of Eden and away from his presence. The whole Bible is the story of God restoring his relationship with human beings.

In last week's discussion, we learned that God promises to take the Israelites as his own people and to be their God (Exod. 20). In Exodus 25–28, he instructs them to build a moveable dwelling place or "tabernacle," so that he can once again dwell with them as he did in Eden. I'd encourage you to read these chapters on your own this week.

The tabernacle will show God's people what heaven is like, so he instructs them to fill it with all kinds of precious objects—altars, a lamp, a basin for washing, and a table for serving bread. Each of these pieces of furniture will remind the people that *a holy God* dwells with them. The most special part of the tent will be called the Most Holy Place, which is separated by a curtain embroidered with cherubim (like the ones guarding the Garden of Eden). Moses is to keep the ark of the covenant with the tablets of the law inside it. God's own presence will reside in the Most Holy Place.

Because the people of Israel are sinful, they cannot come directly into God's presence. God appoints priests and Levites as mediators to bridge the relationship between God and the people. The Levites will care for the tabernacle and all its sacred objects and furniture. The priests will make sacrifices to "atone" for the people, which means to both cleanse and pay for their sin. In this way, God will once again live with his people.

But even as God meets with Moses to reveal his law, the people of Israel show their sinfulness once again. Let's read from Exodus 32 and 34 to see what happens.

Bible Readings

Exodus 32:1–6, 15–29; 34:1–12;
Hebrews 4:14–18; John 1:14-18

Observe

Read Exodus 32:1–6, 15–29. State the who, where, when, and what of the passage.

What problem do the people perceive while Moses is away receiving God's instructions and laws?

Look back at Exodus 24:12. What are the stone tablets? What does Moses do with them in Exodus 32:15–19?

Read Exodus 34:1–12. What does God instruct Moses to do? What does God say he will do?

What are some different ways God describes his character to Moses in Exodus 34:6–7?

 Interpret

Why do you think the people want Aaron to make them an idol? How does this directly contradict God's words in Exodus 20:1–6? (Turn to someone next to you to answer, then report back to the group.)

In Exodus 28, we read God's instructions that Aaron and his sons will be priests set apart to offer sacrifices in the tabernacle. Meanwhile, back down the mountain, the people directly disobey God's commands by asking Aaron to make an idol. How do Aaron and the people's disobedience reflect the sin of Adam and Eve in the garden of Eden (Exod. 32:2–4, 21–24)?

What do you think it means to be a "stiff-necked" people? How do God's actions and words in Exodus 34 demonstrate how he will relate to people who sin against him?

 Apply

In Exodus 25:8, God says that the purpose of the tabernacle is that he may dwell among his people. How does the tabernacle begin to restore what God intended for Adam and Eve in the Garden of Eden?

Just like Adam and Eve, the people of Israel want to worship something they can see and touch (such as a golden calf idol). Because of sin, all human beings have this tendency to put something else in God's rightful place. What are some idols you might be tempted to put in God's place in your life today?

In Exodus 34:6–7, God reveals his gracious character, which is associated with his personal name, Yahweh (usually translated as Lord). How does the character of the Lord God give us confidence that God forgives our sin through the work of Jesus our Lord?

 Connecting the Bible's Big Story

Read Hebrews 4:14–18. What does the author of Hebrews say Jesus does for us? How does Jesus more perfectly fulfill the roles of Moses and Aaron?

If you have time, read John 1:14–18 together.

How do these verses help us understand the big story we see unfolding throughout the Bible?

 Gospel Application

In Exodus 25:8, God had commanded Moses: "Then have them make me a sanctuary, and I will dwell among them." Moses had told the people to bring freewill offerings of gold, silver, bronze, and many other precious materials for the building of the tabernacle. But later, while Moses is on the mountain receiving God's instructions, the people take up an offering to make a *false* god—a golden calf! This story from Exodus 32 shows us Israel's sinfulness before a holy God.

Given Israel's outright rebellion, we might expect that God would have canceled his plan to dwell among them in the tabernacle. But in chapter 34, we see that God remains faithful to his promises, not destroying Israel for their sin. This is a God who is committed to dwelling with his people because he is gracious.

The tabernacle that God instructs Moses to build is only the beginning of God's promises coming true. At just the right time, God comes to earth as a *person*. The apostle John says this about Jesus: "The Word became flesh and made his dwelling among us. We have seen his glory, the glory of the one and only Son, who came from the Father, full of grace and truth" (John 1:14).

Jesus "becomes flesh"—becomes a human being—to rescue God's people from sin through his life, death, and resurrection. And the story of the Bible points forward to the time when Jesus will return so that we can dwell with him.

When you find yourself caught in sin, you can be sure that God will forgive your sin and restore you as you trust him as Lord. He is "the compassionate and gracious God, slow to anger, abounding in love and faithfulness" (Exod. 34:6). In sending Jesus, he has made a way to be *with you* forever.

Additional Bible Readings

Exodus 25:1–40; 28:1–43; John 1:14–18; Hebrews 5:1–10; 1 Peter 2:9–10

Review Old Testament Timeline and Maps

Review the Sinai section on the timeline.
Review the second map, *The Exodus from Egypt*.

Dig Deeper with the *Old Testament Study Guide*

Read the next section of chapter three: Sinai (pp. 69-78).

Bible Study Notes

WEEK 8

Atonement Through Sacrifice

Relationship with God requires atonement through sacrifice.

 Icebreaker Questions

Say your name and briefly share two or three qualities you value most in a friend.

Have you ever needed to repair a friendship when you have hurt someone, or they've hurt you? What can it look like to rebuild trust after an offense?

Today, we'll see how God makes a way for ongoing repair in his relationship with his people.

The Bible's Big Story

- Can anyone remember what the letters in the CASKET acronym stand for?
- We're currently in the part of the biblical story we refer to as SINAI because God gives instructions to his people at Sinai.

- Last week we learned that *God makes a way to dwell with his people, even as they continue to sin against him.*
- This week we're going to discover why ***relationship with God requires atonement through sacrifice.***

Setting the Stage

Relationships are messy. A friend gossips behind your back. Someone cancels you because of your beliefs. You talk back to your parents or another adult. Siblings say mean things to one another. All of these actions and words show that sin marks even our best human relationships. But most of all, our wrongdoing means that there is a break in our relationship with God. We need someone to bring us back into right relationship with him.

Last week, we read that God comes to dwell among his people in the tabernacle—but there is still a problem. Because of the people's sin and rebellion against God, they can't be in his presence. God is *holy*, which is another way of saying he is morally pure and perfect in all his ways. So, he cannot dwell with sin or the impurity that results from it.

But God makes a way to be with his people through the sacrifice of animals in the tabernacle (and later temple). He gives Moses instructions about several different sacrifices for different kinds of sin and impurity. These sacrifices will allow Israel to stay in relationship with him. The Old Testament book of Leviticus outlines the different sacrifices, which Aaron and other priests are to make on behalf of the people. Sometimes the sacrifice ends with a meal that points to the restored relationship. One day each year, on the Day of Atonement, God makes a way to deal with the sins of the whole nation of Israel.

It's important to understand that the blood of animals can't fully pay for sin. Israelite priests keep preparing and offering sacrifices day after day and year after year until God sends a *final* and *better* sacrifice.

Bible Readings

Leviticus 16:1–10, 15–22, 29–34;
Hebrews 10:1–4, 11–18; Revelation 5:11–14

Observe

Read Leviticus 16:1–10, 15–22, 29–34. Why does God say that Aaron and the other priests are not to come into the Most Holy Place any time they choose (vv. 1–2)?

The word "atone" means "to make a ransom payment" for sin (the animal's life is the payment instead of a person's life). The blood of sacrificial animals was used for atonement and purification. Looking through the whole chapter, how many times do you see this word "atonement" used? How many different sacrifices are there?

What happens to the live goat (often called the "scapegoat") and how does this symbolically picture the removal of sin (vv. 7-10)?

Interpret

What does this passage show us about Israel's ongoing problem with sin?

How does the high priest mediate between God and the people in Leviticus 16?

Why do you think God gives such specific instructions about the Day of Atonement?

 Apply

Is it easy or difficult for you to confess your sins to God and ask him for forgiveness? Take time to pray for one another about anything people feel comfortable sharing.

 Connecting the Bible's Big Story

Read Hebrews 10:1–4, 11–18. (If time permits, read Hebrews 10:1–18.)

How does Jesus function as the Great High Priest, mediating between God and Christians today? How does his once-for-all sacrifice deal with our ongoing problem with sin?

Read Revelation 5:11–14. How do these verses help us understand the big story we see unfolding throughout the Bible?

 Gospel Application

Although God's people have promised to keep God's laws and to obey him fully, throughout the Old Testament, we find that they just keep on sinning. The sin nature that began with Adam and Eve is deep in them. No matter how much they think they can follow God, in reality, they are a stiff-necked people (Exod. 32:9).

But God is not finished with Israel! By creating a space to dwell with sinful people (the tabernacle) and by providing a way to deal with sin (the sacrificial system), God keeps his covenant promise to stay in relationship with his people. Some scholars note that Leviticus falls in the middle of the five Books of Moses, with Leviticus 16 at the very center. This placement shows us how important it is to God to forgive and cleanse his people.

You and I have the same problem Israel did. Sin is deep within us. Praise God that he is not finished with us either! Instead, he has given us a fuller and more permanent way to have a relationship with him—his own Son Jesus, who has come to offer "for all time one sacrifice for sins" (Heb. 10:12). Because of Jesus' sinless life in our place and his death on our behalf, we can live in relationship with God in spite of our sin.

The writer to the Hebrews goes on to say that Jesus has "made perfect forever those who are being made holy" (Heb. 10:14). This means that although we are *being* sanctified (made holy) until we see Jesus face to face, we have *already* been justified (declared right with God). Another way to say this is that when God looks at those who are united to Christ by faith, he sees Jesus' perfect life in our place. And when we finally dwell with him forever, we will be holy just like Jesus.

As you think about your life, do you see the ugliness of sin and the way it keeps you from God? Look to Jesus, the spotless lamb of God, crucified for you on the cross. He is the mediator of a new covenant, and his atoning sacrifice covers *every* sin so that you can be with God—now and forever.

Additional Bible Readings

Leviticus 4; 16; Numbers 14; Hebrews 9–10

Review Old Testament Timeline and Maps

Review the Sinai section on the timeline.

Review the second map, *The Exodus from Egypt*. Trace the Israelite journey from the Wilderness of Paran to Kadesh-barnea. After wandering in the wilderness for forty years, they arrive on the Plains of Moab, as they prepare to enter the land by crossing the Jordan River.

Dig Deeper with the *Old Testament Study Guide*

Read the next section of chapter three: SINAI (pp. 78-83).

Bible Study Notes

WEEK 9

Onward Under Joshua

God leads his people onward
to the promised land under Joshua.

Icebreaker Questions

Say your name and briefly tell the group about a big transition you've experienced in your life—maybe a move, family changes, or switching to a new school.

What are some of the challenges that come with changes you or your friends have faced? Are there any positive aspects to some of these life transitions?

Today, we'll read about a moment of transition in the life of God's people as Moses passes the baton of leadership to Joshua.

The Bible's Big Story

- Can anyone remember what the letters in the CASKET acronym stand for?

- This will be our final week in the part of the biblical story we refer to as SINAI because God is leading his people from Sinai to the promised land.
- Last week we learned that *relationship with God requires atonement through sacrifice.*
- This week we're going to discover that ***God leads his people onward to the promised land under Joshua.***

 Setting the Stage

As we pick up the biblical storyline, Israel faces a monumental transition of leadership and location. The people have spent 40 years wandering in the desert. But the distance between Egypt and Canaan is less than 400 miles, about the same distance between New York City and Pittsburgh. It's a journey they likely could have made in a few weeks.

The 40 years of wandering are a consequence of the people's unbelief. When God sent representatives to spy out the land of Canaan, the people had refused to trust God in faith. No one from the older generation will be able to enter the promised land. Instead, God will make good on his promise to their children and grandchildren.

Now, the new generation is encamped east of the Jordan River in a land called Moab, ready to enter the land God is giving them. In the book of Deuteronomy, we read Moses' words to this younger generation as God renews the covenant with them. Although God will not allow Moses to go with them because of his own unbelief (Num. 20:1–13; Deut. 32:51–52), Moses reminds the people that

God will continue to uphold his promises. He urges Israel to keep watch over their lives, loving God, resisting the urge to worship other gods, and obeying all of God's commands.

The last chapter in Deuteronomy records the death of Moses, who has had a unique relationship with the Lord. Now God appoints Joshua as Israel's new leader. Joshua had trusted the Lord when he had spied out the land 40 years earlier, and he will lead the people into Canaan.

Bible Readings

Deuteronomy 4:1–2, 15–20, 25–31;
Joshua 1:1–18; Hebrews 4:8–16

Observe

Read Deuteronomy 4:1–2, 15–20, 25–31. What is the purpose of God's message to the Israelites as they prepare to enter the promised land? (vv. 1–2)

Why does Moses remind the people that they must not worship idols (vv. 15–20)?

What does Moses foresee will happen to God's people in the years to come? How will God continue to be faithful to them even when this happens (vv. 25–31)?

Read Joshua 1:1–18. What promises does God give to Joshua as the people prepare to enter the land of Canaan?

What instructions does God give to the people?

 Interpret

At the end of Joshua 1, the people pledge to do all that the Lord has said. Does this remind you of anything we've seen earlier in the biblical narrative? (Hint: Read Exod. 24:3, which we covered in Week 6.)

The people also promise to obey Joshua "just as we fully obeyed Moses." Did the people actually obey Moses? Do you think they will actually obey Joshua?

 Apply

Who are the spiritual leaders in your life? How do they remind you to stay faithful to God and his Word as you face constant changes in your life?

The apostle Paul said to his followers: "Follow my example, as I follow the example of Christ" (1 Cor. 11:1). What does it look like to follow Jesus as our ultimate leader?

 Connecting the Bible's Big Story

Read Hebrews 4:8–16. How do these verses help us understand the big story we see unfolding throughout the Bible?

 Gospel Application

When God leads his people into Canaan, various people groups have already been living in the land. God had told Abraham hundreds of years earlier that his descendants would not take possession of the land of Canaan until the fourth generation (Gen. 15:13–16). The people living in Canaan are sinful, and their pagan religious practices mean that seven nations will fall under God's judgment through the conquest (Deut. 7:1-6), although in his mercy, God has waited hundreds of years.

This part of Scripture may sound a bit strange to our modern ears because we have seen so much harmful conflict throughout world history. But in the biblical storyline, God is the righteous judge of all the earth, and he holds all nations accountable.

In Joshua 2–6, we read about the conquest of the pagan Canaanite city of Jericho. A non-Israelite woman named Rahab has heard how the God of Israel defeated Egypt. So, she helps some Israelite spies escape from Jericho's king. The spies tell her to hang a scarlet cord in her window so that their army will spare her household when they return, requiring a huge step of faith. Amazingly, this foreign woman, who is identified as a prostitute (or possibly an innkeeper) will become an ancestor of King David, and she is listed in Jesus' own genealogy (Matt. 1:5)! Rahab reminds us that God has always been at work to draw people from all nations into relationship with himself.

Before Joshua dies, God calls him to remind the people again to serve him as their only God: "Throw away the gods your fathers worshiped beyond the Euphrates River and in Egypt, and serve the Lord" (Josh. 24:14b). The people repeatedly insist that they will serve God only (Josh. 24:16–28), but they will fail to keep their promise.

Like Israel, we also struggle to serve the Lord and can easily turn to worship lesser gods (often good things that we put in God's place, like sports, academics, social media, or human relationships). God graciously gives us spiritual leaders—our parents, pastors, and youth ministers—who can help us follow him. Still, what we need most of all is a leader who has the power to save us from sin and death.

Joshua's name ("Yahweh saves") points ahead to *Jesus*, whose name represents the Greek form of Joshua. In an even greater way than Joshua leads Israel, Jesus leads us back into relationship with God the Father through his perfect life, sinless death, and resurrection from the dead. When we face transition or change, Jesus is our constant leader who will never fail us.

Additional Bible Readings

Deuteronomy 15; Joshua 2–3; 24; Hebrews 11:30–34

Review Old Testament Timeline and Maps

Review the SINAI section on the timeline.

Review the third map, *Tribal Allotment of the Promised Land.*

Dig Deeper with the *Old Testament Study Guide*

Read the final section of chapter three: SINAI (pp. 83-91).

Bible Study Notes

WEEK 10

God's Anointed King

God appoints David as his anointed king over Israel.

Icebreaker Questions

Say your name and briefly share something you are planning or looking forward to in the coming months or years.

Has there ever been a time when you had to wait longer than expected to see your plans through? How does it feel when something you're hoping for gets delayed?

In today's passage, we will read about God's good plans for King David, which unfold differently than David expects.

The Bible's Big Story

- Can anyone remember what the letters in the CASKET acronym stand for?
- This is our first week in the part of the biblical story we refer to as KINGS because God appoints a king for Israel through the family line of Judah.

- The picture for the period of KINGS is a crown representing kingship.
- Last week we learned that *God leads his people onward to the promised land under Joshua.*
- This week we're going to discover that ***God appoints David as his anointed king over Israel.***

 Setting the Stage

In the beginning of Israel's story, God is their only king. Still, the people don't want to follow God's rule and for a time everyone "did what he saw fit" (Judg. 21:25). But then God calls a young boy named Samuel to serve in the tabernacle with Eli the priest (1 Sam. 1). Eli's own sons are corrupting the sacrifices and the priesthood itself (1 Sam. 2:12–26). So, God calls Samuel to speak judgment against them (1 Sam. 3).

Meanwhile, the neighboring Philistines defeat Israel in battle and capture the ark of the covenant, taking it to their own territory. Samuel urges Israel to stop worshiping idols and worship God alone. But the Israelites want to be like the nations around them. They beg Samuel for an earthly king to fight their battles.

The Lord tells Samuel the people are not rejecting him as a prophet, but rather, they are rejecting God as their true king. In spite of this, God gives the people the king they want—a warrior named Saul. He *looks* the part, but he does not obey God, so his reign is cut short (1 Chron. 10:13-14). While Saul is still king, God tells Samuel to anoint a young shepherd boy named David from Judah's line in the town of Bethlehem. God's Spirit departs from Saul but is with David. Although he is very young, David defeats a Philistine giant named Goliath (God loves to use youth as part of his plan!).

Saul perceives David as a threat to his throne and eventually seeks to kill him. David hides in the wilderness until Saul dies. Finally, David is anointed king according to God's timing. God grants David military success, and Jerusalem becomes the capital of the kingdom.

Bible Readings

2 Samuel 7; 1 Chronicles 29;
Matthew 2:1–6; Acts 2:24–28

Observe

Read 2 Samuel 7. What does David notice about the tabernacle, and what does he want to do for God?

How does Nathan the prophet initially respond to David's plan? How does he change his mind after hearing from the Lord?

God makes promises to King David that are important for the whole Bible. What promises does God make concerning David's descendant (vv. 12–14)?

Read 1 Chronicles 29. How does David respond when God says that David's son will build the temple instead of him?

What do David's words in vv. 14–16 communicate about how he views his wealth?

Interpret

Even though God says "no" to David's plan of building the temple, he has far better plans for David. What do David's prayers and actions show us about his posture toward the Lord?

Why do you think David rehearses the story of Israel in his prayers?

 Apply

How do David's two prayers remind us of God's covenant and character? (Let's have multiple people share different aspects of who God is.)

When God answers your prayers with a "no," is it easy or difficult for you to trust him and praise him the way David does? Why or why not?

 Connecting the Bible's Big Story

Read Acts 2:24–28. The writers of the New Testament emphasize the connection between Jesus and the line of King David to show that Jesus fulfilled all of God's promises. How is Jesus an even better king than David?

Read Matthew 2:1–6. How do these verses help us understand the big story we see unfolding throughout the Bible?

 Gospel Application

We remember King David for all the ways he served the Lord in his time as king. But it's important to know that David wasn't perfect—far from it.

On one occasion, David commits adultery and gets another man's wife pregnant, and then has her husband killed (2 Sam. 11). But David repents of his sin and experiences God's gracious forgiveness. Despite David's adultery, God remains faithful to his covenant to establish David's throne and the family line of Judah forever. David's son Solomon will build God's "house" (the temple), but God himself will build a "house" for David—an everlasting kingdom and throne.

Still, the reality of David's sin makes us hope for *an even better king,* one who will not look out for his own interests, but for the good of God's people.

Many generations later, this *better* king arrives on the scene: Jesus, the Messiah. Jesus is David's descendant, born in David's hometown of Bethlehem. Before Jesus' birth, his mother, Mary, receives word from an angel that God will give her son "the throne of his father David" and that he will reign forever and "his kingdom will never end" (Luke 1:32–33).

Jesus' arrival points us back to God's plan for his people, to be our *only* king. Like Israel, we tend to look for something or someone to justify us, to make us like those around us. But Jesus is the king we truly need, and he has come to rescue us.

Have you been disappointed when your plans don't unfold as you'd hoped? Remember the covenant God reveals to King David and that God keeps his word even in the face of David's sin. Jesus is God's assurance of his good and gracious plans for your life. When you trust in him, you will not be shaken (Ps. 16:8; Acts 2:25).

Additional Bible Readings

2 Samuel 5; Psalm 2; Luke 1:32–33; Acts 13:22–39

Review Old Testament Timeline and Maps

Review the KINGS section on the timeline.

Review the fourth map, *The United Kingdom*. Notice the expansion of the kingdom that takes place under David (shown in blue) compared to the kingdom ruled by Saul (shown in red).

Dig Deeper with the *Old Testament Study Guide*

Read the first section of chapter four: KINGS: United Monarchy (pp. 93-112).

Bible Study Notes

WEEK 11

Solomon Builds the Temple

King Solomon builds the temple for God's glory.

Icebreaker Questions

Say your name and an accomplishment you're proud of.

Have you ever experienced pressure or disappointment after accomplishing a goal of some kind? Share some examples if you feel comfortable. (For example, you make the team, and now the pressure is on to stay at the top of your game.)

Today we'll read about King Solomon, who receives wisdom from God and builds the temple. Unfortunately, Solomon struggles to stay faithful to God afterward.

The Bible's Big Story

- Can anyone remember what the letters in the CASKET acronym stand for?

- This week we continue in the part of the biblical story we refer to as Kings because God appoints a king for Israel through the family line of Judah.
- Last week we learned that *God appoints David as his anointed king over Israel.*
- This week we're going to discover that ***King Solomon builds the temple for God's glory.***

 Setting the Stage

Last week we read how King David had wanted to build a permanent dwelling place for the Lord to replace the tabernacle. But God told David that his son Solomon would succeed him as king, and that Solomon would build the temple.

When David dies and Solomon receives the throne, the young and inexperienced new king seeks God in prayer. God appears to Solomon in a dream and invites him to ask for whatever he wants the Lord to give him. Solomon confesses his weakness to lead the kingdom, and he asks God to give him wisdom, saying, "So give your servant a discerning heart to govern your people and to distinguish between right and wrong. For who is able to govern this great people of yours?" (1 Kings 3:9).

Solomon's request pleases God, who pledges to give Solomon "a wise and discerning heart," along with wealth, honor, and a long life. Solomon expands the kingdom through numerous military victories, and his reign ushers in a period of prosperity. Even foreign rulers, like the Queen of Sheba, recognize Solomon's wisdom and Israel's expanding kingdom. Most importantly, Solomon builds a temple for the Lord to replace the movable tabernacle, just as God had told David he would.

Bible Readings

2 Chronicles 6:12–17, 36–42; 7:1–10;
1 Corinthians 3:16–17; Revelation 21:22–27

Observe

Read 2 Chronicles 6:12–17, 36–42. What does Solomon say in his prayer about God's character and about his promises to David?

What does Solomon ask the Lord to give him?

How does Solomon describe human sin?

Read 2 Chronicles 7:1–10. State the who, what, when, and where of the passage.

Who is present to witness the dedication of the temple?

Interpret

How do the people respond to seeing God's glorious presence filling the temple?

What do these passages show us about the purpose of the temple?

Apply

We read that the people went home "joyful and glad in heart for the good things the Lord had done" (2 Chron. 7:10). Have you ever been in awe of God's goodness and glory? If so, what was that experience like for you?

 Connecting the Bible's Big Story

Read 1 Corinthians 3:16–17. What does Paul say is true of Christians? What do you think it means that the Church (all people everywhere who follow Jesus) is now the earthly home for God's presence (see also 1 Pet. 2:4–10)?

Read Revelation 21:22–27. How do these verses help us understand the big story we see unfolding throughout the Bible?

 Gospel Application

After Solomon dedicates the temple to the Lord, God speaks to Solomon, confirming his promises to Israel. If God's people repent and turn back to the Lord, he will heal their land. What's more, God pledges to Solomon that he will fulfill his covenant promises to King David, but there's one condition: Solomon must continue to follow God alone. If Solomon and the people turn away from the Lord, then God will allow his temple to be destroyed, and the people will be uprooted from their land.

Sadly, both Solomon and Israel fail to uphold their end of the covenant. The king marries foreign wives, and toward the end of his life he worships their pagan gods. The people also worship the gods of the nations, forsaking the covenant command to love the Lord their God with all their heart, soul, and strength.

As a result of Solomon's idolatry, Israel will eventually be divided into two kingdoms. God will continue his promise to David by preserving the line of Judah as the smaller of the two kingdoms, but it will be only a shadow of the original monarchy. And several hundred years after Solomon's reign, the Babylonians will ransack the temple and bring God's people into exile.

Even so, God has good plans for his people. Generations later, a Son will be born to David's descendants—Jesus from the line of Judah. God comes to dwell with his people once again! Jesus will explain that his own body is the temple of the Lord (John 2:19). Then he will send the Holy Spirit to come and live within all who trust him in faith.

If you have trusted in Jesus as Lord, then God's Spirit now lives within you! Together as Christ's body, we are the new temple of the Lord. One day, we will dwell with him forever. In the meantime, as we struggle with sin, we do not need to perform or measure up in order to get to God. Jesus' work on our behalf is the only performance that is needed when we trust him in faith. Our place with him is secure.

Additional Bible Readings

1 Kings 11; 2 Chronicles 1; 1 Peter 2:4–10

Review Old Testament Timeline and Maps

Review the KINGS section on the timeline.

Review the fourth map, *The United Kingdom*, and notice the expansion of the kingdom that takes place under Solomon.

Dig Deeper with the *Old Testament Study Guide*

Read the last section of chapter four: KINGS: United Monarchy (pp. 113-119).

Bible Study Notes

WEEK 12

Rebellion in the Kingdom

Leaders prompt rebellion, but prophets call people back to the Lord.

Icebreaker Questions

Say your name and share two or three qualities you most admire in a leader.

Why do you think people often follow a bad leader? What is it that draws people to leaders with questionable character?

Today we'll read about major leadership challenges in Israel.

The Bible's Big Story

- Can anyone remember what the letters in the CASKET acronym stand for?
- We are continuing in the part of the biblical story we refer to as KINGS because God appoints a king for Israel through the family line of Judah.

- This week we are studying the northern kingdom of Israel after the monarchy has been divided into two.
- Last week we learned that *King Solomon builds the temple for God's glory.*
- This week we're going to discover that ***leaders prompt rebellion, but prophets call people back to the Lord.***

 Setting the Stage

Last week we read that Solomon builds the temple, but at the end of his life, he worships false gods instead of the Lord. Just as God had promised, Solomon experiences the consequences of his unfaithfulness.

One of his highest-ranking officials, Jeroboam, rebels against Solomon. The prophet Ahijah tells Jeroboam that God will give him ten of the twelve tribes of Israel, forming the northern kingdom (known as Israel). But God will preserve the tribes of Judah and Benjamin, along with the Levites who minister in the temple, as the southern kingdom (known as Judah). A king from David's line will remain on the throne in Jerusalem, beginning with Solomon's son Rehoboam.

Jeroboam sets up two golden calves (like the one God's people made in Exodus) for the people to worship instead of the Lord—one in a town called Bethel and another in a town called Dan. Ahijah the prophet announces God's judgment against Jeroboam for his failure to keep the covenant. Jeroboam's false worship begins a pattern in the northern kingdom of Israel that will continue for over 200 years.

The worst of the northern kings is a man named Ahab, who marries a pagan woman named Jezebel. He builds a temple to a foreign god called Baal and he sets up pagan cult objects. During Ahab's reign,

God raises up the prophet Elijah to announce God's judgment against Ahab, his sons, and the gods they worship. Elijah challenges 450 prophets of Baal to a cosmic duel. The Lord proves that he is the one true God by sending fire on an altar doused in water. Ahab and his wife Jezebel both die gruesome deaths, but wickedness continues among Israel's kings.

God raises up the prophets Hosea and Amos to speak his words to the people as their true leader and king. Hosea exposes the people's ongoing sin of worshiping gods other than the Lord, and Amos speaks to the injustices the people in the north are committing against one another.

Bible Readings

1 Kings 16:29–34; Hosea 1:1–11;
Luke 10:29–37; John 4:3–30

Observe

Read 1 Kings 16:29–34. How does this passage describe the wickedness of King Ahab?

What are the "sins of Jeroboam" that Ahab continues (see 1 Kings 12:25–33)?

Read Hosea 1:1–11. What is something God tells Hosea to do that might seem strange to you?

What odd names does God tell Hosea to give his children? You can reference 2 Kings 9:1–13 for the background on the name Jezreel.

 Interpret

There are several cases in the Old Testament when God asks a prophet to act out a picture of the prophecy he speaks to the people. How is the northern kingdom of Israel behaving like a prostitute? How is God's relationship with Israel like a husband who remains faithful to an unfaithful spouse?

Summarize the incredible promise God gives Israel through Hosea.

 Apply

How does the wickedness of northern kings like Ahab show us our need for a good and righteous king?

The kings and the people of Israel all struggled with the sin of *idolatry*—elevating something or someone instead of God. What idols does our own culture tend to worship? What are some things you tend to put before God in your own life?

 Connecting the Bible's Big Story

Read Luke 10:29–37. The divided kingdom led to continued animosity between the north and south, even in Jesus' day. How does Jesus challenge the religious leaders in Jerusalem to think about his kingdom? Who is Jesus' kingdom for?

Read John 4:3–30. How do these verses help us understand the big story we see unfolding throughout the Bible?

 Gospel Application

When the people of Israel first asked God to give them a king like the other nations, he warned them about the costs of such a king (1 Sam. 8). Now, as the northern kings serve their own interests instead of God's, the people begin to experience that cost more fully. But instead of turning from their sin and renewing their covenant relationship with the Lord, the people follow the wicked ways of these human rulers. Because of the people's ongoing sin, God will raise up the nation of Assyria to conquer the northern kingdom in 722 BC. This fulfills the curses associated with disobedience in Deuteronomy 27–28.

But even in the face of the people's outright rebellion, God raises up prophets to call his people to return to him and worship him alone. The prophets announce that judgment is coming if the people do not repent, and they offer the hope of restoration for those who follow the Lord.

At just the right time, God sends his Son, Jesus, as the fulfillment of all these prophecies. Jesus is the true king of Israel and the redeemer of all who trust him in faith. He comes to take the curses of the covenant on himself, dying in our place. In doing so, he restores those who trust in him so that we can serve him. The New Testament makes clear that Jesus is the king for all people, including those from the northern kingdom, like the Samaritan woman at the well.

When you look at the world's leaders and feel disappointed, remember that Jesus is the true and better leader our world needs. Because he lived the perfect life, died in your place, and rose again from the dead, you can trust and follow him today.

Additional Bible Readings

1 Kings 14:17–20; 15:25–30; 2 Kings 9:1–13; 17:1–41

Review Old Testament Timeline and Maps

Review the KINGS section on the timeline.

Review the fifth map, *The Divided Kingdom*. Identify the southern kingdom in blue and the northern kingdom in red. Identify the northern cities of Samaria, Dan, and Bethel.

Review the sixth map, *The Assyrian* and *Babylonian Empires*. Notice the vastness of the Assyrian Empire. The exiles are sent east to Assyria, and foreigners are brought into Samaria.

Dig Deeper with the *Old Testament Study Guide*

Read sections from chapter five: KINGS: The Northern Kingdom (pp. 121-134, 139-145, 150-152).

Bible Study Notes

WEEK 13

Davidic Kings Rule Over Judah

God keeps his promises as kings from David's line rule over Judah.

Icebreaker Questions

Say your name and share a person (or group of people) whom you would ask for advice.

Has there ever been a time you regretted not taking someone's good advice? Why do you think it can be so difficult to receive wisdom from others in the moment?

Today we'll see how the kings of Judah often rejected feedback from their advisors and from the prophets.

The Bible's Big Story

- Can anyone remember what the letters in the CASKET acronym stand for?

- We are continuing in the part of the biblical story we refer to as KINGS because God appoints an earthly king for Israel through the family line of Judah. This week we are studying the southern kingdom of Judah where kings from David's line continue to rule.
- Last week we learned that *leaders prompt rebellion, but prophets call people back to the Lord.*
- This week we're going to discover that ***God keeps his promises as kings from David's line rule over Judah.***

 Setting the Stage

In our reading today, we'll backtrack several years from last week's passages so that we can trace what happens to God's people in the southern kingdom of Judah. This is where Solomon's son, Rehoboam, reigns as king. His reign represents a continuation of God's promise to David that his family would rule over the kingdom.

Unlike Solomon, who looked to the Lord for wisdom early in his leadership, Rehoboam rejects the good advice of his advisors, leading to the division of the kingdom, as we talked about last week. Worse than that, Rehoboam rejects the Lord's own counsel, establishing worship of false gods like the nations. God punishes Rehoboam for his wickedness, but David's family line continues because God is faithful to his covenant with David.

Throughout the generations of the southern kingdom, there are several kings who follow God and seek to restore proper worship in the temple. But other kings of Judah lead the people into idolatry, just as the kings in the north are doing. God raises up prophets to speak messages of judgment, calling the kings and the people to repentance.

The same prophets also speak God's promises of hope for the future, if only the people and their leaders will turn back to the Lord.

Two kings who serve the Lord faithfully are Rehoboam's grandson, Asa and his son Jehoshaphat. Asa trusts in God and reduces pagan worship, and Jehoshaphat also trusts in God and makes many positive reforms of Judah's worship. Still, neither of them fully abolishes pagan worship. As we study the southern kingdom, we will find that even the best of Judah's kings will fail in one way or another.

Bible Readings

2 Chronicles 15:1–19; 20:1–30;
1 Corinthians 1:18–25; Ephesians 6:10–20

Read 2 Chronicles 15:1–19. Share the who, what, when, and where of this passage.

What advice does Azariah give Asa?

How does Asa respond to Azariah's counsel about idols? How would you describe this early period in his reign?

Read 2 Chronicles 20:1–30. How does Jehoshaphat respond to the news of the Edomite army's advance against Judah?

Describe what happens to a Levite named Jahaziel and the advice he gives Jehoshaphat.

How does God accomplish Judah's victory over their enemies? What does Jehoshaphat's army have to do (vv. 17, 21–22)?

Interpret

What do you think Azariah means when he says "for a long time, Israel was without the true God" (2 Chron. 15:3)? Thinking about our Casket timeline, what period of Israel's history might he be referencing?

Name some different examples of Jehoshaphat's trust in the Lord (2 Chron. 20).

How does God use Azariah and Jahaziel to advise Asa and Jehoshaphat? What do the responses of the two kings show us about their dependence on the Lord?

Apply

It can be tricky to know whose advice to take. Do you think we can know whether wisdom is from God or not? If so, how?

How can we help each other to become people who trust God and seek his wisdom in our lives?

Read 1 Corinthians 1:18–25. What do you think it means that Christ is "the power of God and the wisdom of God" (v. 24)?

Read Ephesians 6:10–20. How do these verses help us understand the big story we see unfolding throughout the Bible?

Gospel Application

Following the relatively good kings Asa and Jehoshaphat, Judah's history sees many more kings who do evil and rebel against the Lord.

Several generations after Jehoshaphat, we meet a king named Uzziah. He initially blesses the kingdom, but later wrongly asserts himself as a priest in the temple, and God punishes him. In the year Uzziah dies, God raises up a prophet named Isaiah, who has a vision of the Lord's *holiness,* a term expressing that God is set apart in absolute moral purity. Isaiah tells the people they have become deaf and blind like the idols they worship, but if they return to worshiping the Lord, God will restore them.

Another king, Ahaz, goes down in history as one of Judah's worst. He engages not only in idolatry but also in the deplorable ancient practice of child sacrifice as part of worshiping false gods. Ahaz leads the people to worship Baal, just like Ahab did in Israel. When the kingdom of Judah is invaded, Ahaz ignores Isaiah's prophecy and makes a deal with the wicked kingdom of Assyria instead.

God allows kings from the line of Judah to continue ruling the southern kingdom, but none of them is the king God's people truly need. When Jesus, the "son of David" is born hundreds of years later, he reveals himself as the true King of Israel and of the whole world. Jesus himself is "the power of God and the wisdom of God" (1 Cor. 1:24). He alone is the conquering King, who wages war "against the powers of this dark world and against the spiritual forces of evil in the heavenly realms" (Eph. 6:12) by paying the penalty for our sin on the cross.

We all find ourselves needing power and wisdom as we live in this broken world. Look no further than to Jesus Christ, who died for you and now reigns in heaven with God the Father.

Additional Bible Readings

1 Kings 12:1–24; 14:21–31; 2 Chronicles 14:1–15; 28:1–27

Review Old Testament Timeline and Maps

Review the Kings section on the timeline.

Review the fifth map, *The Divided Kingdom*. Notice the reduced southern kingdom during this period in comparison to the much larger kingdom during the time of David and Solomon.

Dig Deeper with the *Old Testament Study Guide*

Read the first section of chapter six: Kings: The Southern Kingdom Part 1 (pp. 153-173).

Bible Study Notes

WEEK 14

God Judges and Restores

God judges the southern kingdom of Judah, but he will one day restore his people.

 Icebreaker Questions

Say your name and share about something broken that you'd like to see rebuilt or renewed.

We tend to love stories about broken things being restored, whether it's a relationship, an old house, a kingdom fallen to evil, or an athletic team. Can you think of a restoration story you enjoy? What is it about this theme that is so captivating?

Our passages today highlight promises God makes to his people to restore the broken kingdoms of Israel and Judah.

 The Bible's Big Story

- Can anyone remember what the letters in the CASKET acronym stand for?

- We are continuing in the part of the biblical story we refer to as KINGS because God appoints an earthly king for Israel through the family line of Judah. Again, this week we are studying the southern kingdom of Judah where kings from David's line continue to rule.
- Last week we learned that *God keeps his promise as kings from David's line rule over Judah.*
- This week we're going to discover that ***God judges the southern kingdom of Judah, but he will one day restore his people.***

 Setting the Stage

As we continue our survey of the southern kingdom, you might be growing weary of hearing about the wicked kings who rebel against the Lord. Can you imagine how God felt as he dealt with the generations of sin? Still, he did not give up on his people.

In the midst of many bad kings in Judah, there are a few who do what is right. Hezekiah renews the covenant with God by removing the "high places" (sites of idol worship), cleansing the temple, and restoring the Passover. Some from the northern tribes even repent from evil, and Hezekiah prays for them. When the Assyrian king taunts Hezekiah, he remains faithful to God and calls out to him in prayer. Isaiah encourages Hezekiah to hold a fast, and the Lord sends a single angel to defeat the Assyrian army.

Hezekiah's son Manasseh rebuilds the altars to Baal and engages in both witchcraft and child sacrifice. He even puts an idol in the temple. God allows the king of Assyria to conquer Manasseh, leading him to Babylon with a ring through his nose (a dehumanizing practice done to one's enemy). While in captivity, Manasseh humbles himself and prays to the Lord. In answer to his prayer, God brings him back to Jerusalem. Manasseh then tears down the old idols. Sadly, Manasseh's son Amon brings idolatry and false worship back into Judah.

Amon's son Josiah is faithful to God and begins to rid the land of false worship. The law of Moses has been lost for many years, but a priest finds it during Josiah's reign. A prophetess called Huldah interprets the law for Josiah, saying that God will judge Judah for worshiping other gods. Josiah renews the covenant and restores right worship—but the four kings who come after him are evil kings who fail to repent.

Today we'll read from Isaiah and Micah, two prophets God anointed to speak his words to sinful Judah during this time.

Bible Readings

Isaiah 6:1–13; Micah 6:1–16; 7:18–20;
Matthew 13:1–17; Luke 4:14–21

Observe

Read Isaiah 6:1–13. Where does Isaiah's vision take him, and what does he see there?

What do the seraphim (heavenly creatures) do to cleanse Isaiah's sin?

Read Micah 6:1–16 and 7:18–20. The prophets are known for using strong language to express the sinfulness of human beings and the righteous judgment of God. What images in Micah 6 stand out to you?

What does the Lord remind his people that he has done for them? How does he describe their behavior in response?

 Interpret

How would you summarize the message God gives Isaiah?

How would you summarize the message God gives Micah?

What future assurance does God give his people through these two prophets? (Hint: See if there is anything in Mic. 7:18–20 that helps you understand Isaiah 6:13).

 Apply

What does it tell us about God's character that he both judges sin *and* shows mercy? How can God take sin seriously, while still fulfilling his promises to his people?

 Connecting the Bible's Big Story

Read Matthew 13:1–17. How do Jesus' words draw on the prophecy in Isaiah 6:9–10? How do the disciples demonstrate that their eyes and ears are open to Jesus (Matt. 13:10–17)?

What are some questions about faith, the Bible, or God's character that you could bring to Jesus to demonstrate that your eyes and ears are open?

Read Luke 4:14–21. How do these verses help us understand the big story we see unfolding throughout the Bible?

 Gospel Application

The saga of the southern kingdom reads a little like a Tolkien novel or a story from the Marvel Universe: Good and evil war against one another in the form of world empires and fallen kings. It's hard to imagine how God will intervene to restore his rebellious people—but that's exactly what he promises to do.

As Judah's human kings continue to struggle to obey the Lord and rid the land of idolatry, God sends prophets to represent him. Isaiah and Micah bring a message of judgment against Judah: The people have turned away from the Lord and have become deaf and dumb like the idols they worship (Isa. 6:9–10). They have been dishonest, violent, and deceitful to one another (Mic. 6:10–12).

Still, the prophets also promise something hopeful: A *remnant* (a smaller portion of the people) will turn from wickedness to seek the one true God (Isa. 6:13; Mic. 7:18). Through this minority who trust in the Lord, he will fulfill all the promises he has made.

The restoration we see during the reigns of Hezekiah and Josiah is just a small taste of what God will one day do for his people. He is preparing to set a king on the throne who will reign forever, perfectly obeying God the Father and doing his will (John 8:29). Jesus reveals the mystery of God's kingdom to those whose ears, eyes, and hearts are open to him (Matt. 13:11–12).

Because of God's deep love for his people and his commitment to send Jesus, *restoration is coming.* Even more than in a fantasy novel or a superhero movie, the perfectly good and true Son of God will come to save the day. When your life feels broken by sin—whether yours or that of others—remember Jesus, who comes to proclaim good news to the poor, freedom for prisoners, sight for the blind, and God's favor to all who love him (Isa. 61:1–3).

Additional Bible Readings

2 Chronicles 33–34; Isaiah 1:1–31; 6:1–13

Review Old Testament Timeline and Maps

Review the Kings section on the timeline.

Review the fifth map, *The Divided Kingdom*, and the sixth map, *The Assyrian and Babylonian Empires*. Identify the cities of Lachish and Jerusalem, and note the vast Assyrian Empire.

Dig Deeper with the *Old Testament Study Guide*

Read the final section of chapter six: Kings: The Southern Kingdom Part 1(pp. 174-183).

Bible Study Notes

WEEK 15

Judah's Unrepentant Sin

The kings and people of Judah do not repent but keep sinning.

 Icebreaker Questions

Say your name and share a time when you felt "stuck" in some way. Maybe it was in a class, a friendship, or a habit you just couldn't break (like arguing with a sibling or being on your phone until late in the night).

How does it feel to realize that you're stuck in an old pattern that you can't break? What do you do to try to change?

Today we'll continue studying the history of Israel's southern kingdom, Judah. We'll see how the people and their leaders are stuck in a pattern of sinning against God and each other.

 The Bible's Big Story

- Can anyone remember what the letters in the CASKET acronym stand for?
- We are continuing in the part of the biblical story we refer to as KINGS because God appoints an earthly king for Israel through the

family line of Judah. Again, this week we are studying the southern kingdom of Judah where David's descendants continue to rule.

- Last week we learned that *God judges the southern kingdom of Judah, but will one day restore his people.*
- This week we're going to discover that ***the kings and people of Judah do not repent but keep sinning.***

Setting the Stage

Following King Josiah's reforms in Jerusalem, the kings get worse and worse, and God's people continue to follow them into sin and idolatry. In Jeremiah 7 and 11, the prophet gives a strong warning: If the people continue to worship other gods and to mistreat one another, God will allow foreigners to take Judah from the land, just as Israel has been exiled in the north. God will even allow the temple to be destroyed. And this is exactly what happens.

After Josiah dies, his son Jehoahaz becomes king. But Pharaoh Neco takes him away to Egypt and makes his brother Jehoiakim king over Judah. While Jehoiakim is on the throne, King Nebuchadnezzar of Babylon defeats Egypt and wins control over Judah in 605 BC. He deports the prophet Daniel and other officials to Babylon. The Babylonians also steal many of the sacred objects from the temple.

A few years later in 597 BC, while Jehoiakim's son Jehoiachin is king, Nebuchadnezzar carries out a second deportation, bringing Jehoiachin, the prophet Ezekiel, and other important citizens to Babylon. Jehoiachin's uncle, Zedekiah, becomes king, but like those before him, he sins against the Lord and refuses to listen to the prophets. When he rebels against Nebuchadnezzar, the Babylonians destroy Jerusalem and the temple. They show no mercy, killing Judah's leaders and others, and taking the remaining people into exile in 586 BC.

Through all of these sad events, the prophets continue to speak God's words to the people. This week we'll read some messages of hope that the prophets Jeremiah and Joel give to the people as they face exile.

Bible Readings

Jeremiah 31:27–34; 33:14–18; Joel 2;
Matthew 21:8–11; Acts 2:1–13

Observe

Read Jeremiah 31:27–34 and 33:14–18. What does God promise to do for both Israel and Judah in 31:31–34?

How is the *new* covenant different from the covenant God made with Israel at Mount Sinai (vv. 31–34)?

What does God promise his people in 33:14–18?

Read Joel 2. Have a few people volunteer to read aloud—or you could read one section at a time, following the outline of the "observe" questions below.

How does Joel describe "the Day of the LORD" in vv. 1–11?

What does Joel instruct the people to do in vv. 12–17?

What does the Lord promise to do for the people who return to him in vv. 18–32?

 Interpret

Why do you think God allows foreign nations to conquer his people and destroy the temple?

Based on the passages from Jeremiah and Joel, how would you summarize the message of these southern prophets at the start of the exile?

 Apply

What does the message of these two teach us about God's character? How do his justice and mercy operate together?

How does Joel urge the people to deal with their sin habit (Joel 2:13)? When we are caught in a pattern of sin, what does God ask us to do?

 Connecting the Bible's Big Story

Read Acts 2:1–13. How does God's gift of the Holy Spirit fulfill the words of Joel 2:28–32? (If time permits, continue reading Acts 2:14–24, where Peter quotes Joel.)

Read Matthew 21:8–11. How do these verses help us understand the big story we see unfolding throughout the Bible?

 Gospel Application

God allows his people to be carried off into exile in a foreign land, but he is not finished with them. He will maintain his promise to have a king from the line of Judah on the throne and a priest to mediate between God and his people (Jer. 33:17–18). One day, God will send his own Son to fulfill these roles. Jesus will be the ultimate prophet, the perfect high priest, and the eternal king of his people.

It's tempting for us to imagine that we would somehow respond differently to God and his prophets than the people of Judah did. But the reality is, all human beings have a deep problem with sin. The story of the southern kingdom's fall reminds us of our own need for a Savior.

God's promise of a new covenant through Jeremiah is the good news that you and I need, just as much as Judah did. Just like those people so long ago, we can easily give our hearts to things that are not God (idols). We, too, struggle to obey the Lord and to act with justice. No matter how hard we try to break our patterns of sin, we find ourselves still doing the things we don't want to do (Rom. 7:15–23). But through the work of Christ, God forgives us and remembers our sin no more (Jer. 31:34; Rom. 7:24–25)! He has written his law on our hearts and has made a way for us to personally know him by sending his Spirit to dwell within us (Jer. 31:33-34).

If you find yourself "stuck" in a pattern of sin, remember that our God is "gracious and compassionate, slow to anger and abounding in love, and he relents from sending calamity" (Joel 2:13). Like the kings of Judah, we are not able to fix or change ourselves (Gal. 3:10–11). But God is committed to saving us by the work of his Son on our behalf. Return to him with all your heart, and see what he will do.

Additional Bible Readings

2 Chronicles 36; Jeremiah 7; 11:1–11

Review Old Testament Timeline and Maps

Review the KINGS section on the timeline.

Review the sixth map, *The Assyrian and Babylonian Empires.* Note the vast Babylonian Empire, and how far the city of Babylon is from Jerusalem.

Dig Deeper with the *Old Testament Study Guide*

Read chapter seven: Kings: The Southern Kingdom Part 2 (pp. 185-212).

Bible Study Notes

WEEK 16

Exile to Babylon

God allows his people to experience exile in Babylon.

Icebreaker Questions

Say your name and talk about a time you had a change of heart. (For example, you started cheering for a different sports team, or you became friends with someone you previously couldn't stand.)

Has there ever been a time when you realized your heart had grown hard toward someone in your life—or even toward God?

In our passages today, we'll see that God's people need more than a change of heart—they need God to give them a new heart so that they can trust in him.

The Bible's Big Story

- Can anyone remember what the letters in the CASKET acronym stand for?
- We begin the part of the biblical story called EXILE because the Babylonians take God's people into captivity.

- The picture for the period of Exile is a bird of prey representing the curses of the covenant.
- Last week we learned that *the kings and people of Judah do not repent but keep sinning.*
- This week we're going to discover that ***God allows his people to experience exile in Babylon.***

 Setting the Stage

Last week, we learned that King Nebuchadnezzar conquers Judah and brings many of the kingdom's citizens and leaders to live in Babylon. These events mirror the northern kingdom's exile to Assyria. In Judah, the Babylonians also ransack the temple—the people's pride and the place of God's presence—and then destroy it.

While Judah is exiled in Babylon, God continues to speak through the prophet Jeremiah. He also speaks through two other prophets, Daniel and Ezekiel. You may remember that Daniel is among the first to be deported to Babylon, and Ezekiel is part of the second group.

Ezekiel's ministry begins just before the exile, when God gives him an incredible vision of the Lord's glory. Ezekiel speaks God's words to the people, reminding them how great God is, and urging them to repent (turn away) from their sin. Ezekiel has a vision of God's glory departing from the temple in Jerusalem—a sign of the curses God had promised to send if his people did not remain true to the covenant. The people have worshiped false gods, sacrificed their children to idols, and mistreated the poor, the widow, and the orphan. Now God will allow them to experience the consequences of their sin. Still, God will not abandon his people forever, as we will see in Ezekiel 36.

When Daniel arrives in Babylon, Nebuchadnezzar brings him and other young men from high-ranking Israelite families into a special training program. From the start, Daniel and his three friends continue to worship God and obey his commands, even while in the king's service. The Lord gives Daniel the ability to interpret the king's dreams. We'll read about one of his dreams in Daniel 7.

Bible Readings

Ezekiel 36:22–38; Daniel 7:1–18;
Mark 13:26–27; 14:53–65

Observe

Read Ezekiel 36:22–38. What does God say he will do for his people? (Let's have multiple people answer.)

Why does God say he will do these things?

Read Daniel 7:1–18. Describe each of the beasts in Daniel's vision (vv. 1–8).

How does Daniel describe the "Ancient of Days" in vv. 8–9 and 13–14? Who is he?

How does the "Ancient of Days" interpret the vision for Daniel?

Interpret

How does the "Ancient of Days" show that he is more powerful than the four beasts of Daniel 7?

Turn to someone next to you and try to summarize what new things God promises to do for his people in each of these passages. Then report back to the larger group.

How do you think the promise of a new Spirit within God's people (Ezek. 36) and an everlasting kingdom (Dan. 7) fit together in God's story?

 Apply

Take a moment and reflect personally (or share with the person next to you): Have you trusted in Jesus and received the gifts God promises his people (a new heart and God's Spirit)? If you have, where do you still need God to soften your heart toward him? If you have not yet trusted in Jesus, what is keeping you from doing that now?

 Connecting the Bible's Big Story

Read Mark 14:53–65. What is Jesus claiming about himself in this passage?

Why do you think the religious leaders respond to Jesus' words the way they do?

Read Mark 13:26–27. How do these verses help us understand the big story we see unfolding throughout the Bible?

 Gospel Application

The period of the exile represents an all-time low for God's people. They are taken from the land God promised to give them and are held captive by the Babylonians. They need a new heart and a new way of relating to God.

Even in exile, God continues to speak to his people. Through Ezekiel, God gives a series of incredible promises: God will restore his people to their land. He will cleanse them of their sin and their idols. He will remove their hearts of stone and give them hearts of flesh. He will put his own Spirit in them to help them keep his commands. And through Daniel, God promises a future that will be radically different from their present reality: He will establish his everlasting kingdom, one that will surpass all earthly powers—*forever*.

Jesus fulfills all of these promises: He cleanses us of sin (1 John 1:7) and restores our relationship with God. He removes our hearts of stone and gives us the Holy Spirit to live within us so that we can follow him (John 16:7–15). In fulfillment of Daniel 7, Jesus identifies himself as the Son of Man (Luke 9:22). He reveals that he is the true King who will rule over God's kingdom forever when he returns to earth to make all things right. Those who trust in Jesus will enter the new Jerusalem, the heavenly city, and will dwell with him forever (Rev. 21:2).

Maybe you find yourself in an all-time low, struggling with sin or experiencing the harmful effects of others' sin. If so, then remember what God promises to do for his people. Remember and give thanks for the new heart God gives those who trust in the work of Christ. Be encouraged, knowing that God's kingdom is above all earthly ones and Jesus is the everlasting king.

Additional Bible Readings

Ezekiel 1; 20:1–32; Daniel 1

Review Old Testament Timeline and Maps

Review the Exile section on the timeline.

Review the sixth map, *The Assyrian and Babylonian Empires*. Notice the extent of the Babylonian Empire and the location of the exiles in Babylon.

Dig Deeper with the *Old Testament Study Guide*
Read chapter eight: Exile (pp. 213-245).

Bible Study Notes

WEEK 17

Return, Rebuild, and Restore

By God's grace the exiles return to Jerusalem to rebuild and restore it.

Icebreaker Questions

Say your name and briefly share a time when you have been glad for a new beginning.

Many people look forward to the beginning of a new calendar year or school year to establish new habits. What is it about a fresh start that makes us feel so hopeful?

This week we'll see how God brings his people back into the land, giving them a new start and yet another opportunity to serve him alone.

The Bible's Big Story

- Can anyone remember what the letters in the CASKET acronym stand for?

- Today we begin the part of the biblical story called TEMPLE because the exiles go home to Jerusalem to rebuild the temple and the city.
- The picture for the period of TEMPLE represents the rebuilt temple after the exile.
- Last week we learned that *God allows his people to experience exile in Babylon.*
- This week we're going to discover that ***by God's grace the exiles return to Jerusalem to rebuild and restore it.***

 Setting the Stage

A few years before the exile, the prophet Jeremiah had announced that God's people would remain in captivity for 70 years (Jer. 25:11-12). Now, at the end of those years, King Cyrus of Persia defeats Babylon and issues a decree that allows the exiles to return to Jerusalem. He instructs them to rebuild the temple, fulfilling one of Isaiah's prophecies. That a foreign king allows God's people to return to Jerusalem reminds us that God can use *anyone* to accomplish his purposes.

Among the first exiles to return home are people from the southern tribes of Judah and Benjamin, along with Levites, and people from the northern tribes of Ephraim and Manasseh. The inclusion of both north and south shows that God's people will once again be united. Together, the people build an altar for sacrifice and make offerings to the Lord. Then they stop the work of rebuilding due to opposition from people in neighboring regions.

God raises up the prophets Haggai and Zechariah to encourage the people in the rebuilding project. Haggai calls the people to prioritize building God's house over their own comfort and safety. And Zechariah shares visions from the Lord, announcing God's plan to dwell with his people once again. Amazingly, God's people finally complete the temple.

A few years later, back in Babylon, God raises up a priest named Ezra, who devotes himself to studying God's Word. King Artaxerxes of Persia sends Ezra back to Jerusalem with a group of exiles, many of whom are also priests. When they arrive, Ezra is disturbed to see that many of the Israelites, including some of his fellow priests, have married foreigners who do not follow the one true God—something God has told them not to do.

Bible Readings

Ezra 9:1–15; Haggai 2:1–9; Zechariah 9:9–10;
Matthew 21:1–9; John 2:13–22

Observe

Read Haggai 2:1–9. Give the who, what, when, and where of the passage.

What hopeful promise does God give the returned exiles as they rebuild the temple?

Read Ezra 9:1–15. What does Ezra observe in the temple, and how does he respond (vv. 1–5)?

How does Ezra describe the people's sin in his prayer (vv. 6–15)?

 Interpret

Why does God remind his people of the way he brought them up from Egypt (Hag. 2:5)? How does he want this reminder to strengthen the exiles as they rebuild the temple?

What was the purpose of the tabernacle that came before Solomon's temple? (Hint: Look back at Exod. 25:8 and 29:44–46.) How does Haggai express the ultimate goal of the new temple?

Why is it a problem for God's people to intermarry with women from foreign nations after they return to Israel and rebuild the temple? (Hint: Read Ezra 9:10–12 and look up Deut. 7:1–6.)

 Apply

Have you ever needed a fresh start with the Lord? This could involve renewing a friendship, prioritizing time in God's Word, or perhaps even breaking a habit like cheating. Is there an area of your life where you'd like to begin again now? Share if you feel comfortable.

How should God's commands about intermarriage (i.e., marrying someone who does not follow the true God) influence the way we think about dating relationships both now and in the future?

 Connecting the Bible's Big Story

Read Haggai 2:7–9 and John 2:13–22. How do Haggai and Jesus each describe the restored temple? What do you think Jesus is teaching about himself?

Read Zechariah 9:9–10 and Matthew 21:1–9. How do these verses help us to understand the big story we see unfolding throughout the Bible?

 Gospel Application

After Ezra's prayer of confession, the people gather around him and publicly confess their sin to the Lord (Ezra 10). With the temple rebuilt, the people are able to offer sacrifices once again (Ezra 6:14–18). Sadly, the Bible does not describe God's glory returning to fill the rebuilt temple. This reminds us that God's restoration promises announced by his prophets have not yet been fully realized in the Old Testament. As the story continues, God's people will demonstrate that they still need the kind of heart change the earlier prophets described (see Jer. 31; Ezek. 36).

As the people rebuild the city of Jerusalem, God is doing an even greater work *to rebuild a people* who trust in him and follow his ways. God's intervention to rescue his people will ultimately become clear when Jesus rides a donkey into the city of Jerusalem, showing himself to be the humble king Zechariah described. Jesus is also the true and better temple, fulfilling God's promise to come and dwell with his people.

Our sin means we need a fresh start—and this is just what Jesus offers us when we come to him in faith. Like the exiles, we need God's work in our lives every day. If you find yourself feeling apathetic about the things of God or you know you are actively disobeying God's commands, ask him to work in your heart to help you seek him and start again. He is the one who rebuilds and restores his people. And by God's grace, our humble king Jesus leads us into God's presence.

Additional Bible Readings

Ezra 1:1–11; 6:14–18; Haggai 2:1–9; Zechariah 2:10–11

Review Old Testament Timeline and Maps

Review the TEMPLE section on the timeline.

Review the seventh map, *The Persian Empire*.

Dig Deeper with the *Old Testament Study Guide*

Read the first section of chapter nine: TEMPLE (pp. 247-262).

Bible Study Notes

WEEK 18

Walls Rebuilt, Covenant Renewed

God's people rebuild the walls of Jerusalem, and the covenant is renewed.

Icebreaker Questions

Say your name and briefly share about someone who encourages you when you're down.

What are some of the times when you most need to be encouraged? Have you ever been discouraged spiritually and needed reassurance that God is still with you?

At the end of the Old Testament, God's people are still struggling to trust and obey him. It's not the most uplifting scene. And yet, we will see how God continues to pursue his people.

 The Bible's Big Story

- Can anyone remember what the letters in the CASKET acronym stand for?
- Today we continue the part of the biblical story called TEMPLE because the exiles go home to Jerusalem to rebuild the temple and the city.
- Last week we learned that *by God's grace the exiles return to Jerusalem to rebuild and restore it.*
- This week we're going to discover that ***God's people rebuild the walls of Jerusalem, and the covenant is renewed.***

 Setting the Stage

Our reading this week marks the end of the story of God's people in the Old Testament. A man named Nehemiah, a cupbearer to King Artaxerxes of Persia, hears an upsetting report—the walls of Jerusalem remain in ruins. Nehemiah fasts from food, mourns for his people, and repents for their collective sins. Then he asks Artaxerxes for permission to return to Jerusalem. Artaxerxes agrees, sending Nehemiah with letters of authorization that allow for safe travel and the provision of lumber for the walls, and with the protection of his royal cavalry.

When Nehemiah arrives in Jerusalem, he rides around the city examining the walls and finds them to be in worse condition than he had imagined. He tells the city officials that God has been with him and has provided for God's people. A group joins Nehemiah and begins rebuilding the walls, but foreign leaders quickly oppose them. Still, God is with the builders as they pray, and they complete the project in record time. Nehemiah courageously speaks to his own people, urging the wealthy to stop taking advantage of the poor. He even refuses to take a governor's allowance for himself.

After the completion of the walls, Ezra the priest reads the Law of Moses before a gathering of the city's people. The Levites explain what he reads so that everyone can understand. When they hear God's Word, the people repent from sin and renew the covenant. God has been gracious to them, even when they have been far from him, rebelling against him. We'll read the Levites' prayer for the people in Nehemiah 9.

During this same period, God raises up Malachi as a prophet to speak his words to the people. Malachi hears the people's complaints about the difficulties of life in Jerusalem. He tells the people in no uncertain terms that *they* are the problem. The priests have become corrupt and have dishonored God in his own temple. The people have failed to walk in God's ways. God will come to his people, bringing judgment if they do not turn away from sin and return to him.

Bible Readings

Nehemiah 9; Malachi 4;
Matthew 3:1–12; Luke 24:13–27

Observe

Read Nehemiah 9. What parts of God's story with his people do the Levites recall in their prayer?

How do the Levites describe God's people (vv. 16–18, 26–29)? How do they describe God's character?

Read Malachi 4. What does Malachi say will happen on the Day of the Lord? How will God deal differently with evildoers and with those who follow him?

Whom will God send before the Day of the Lord? What will his purpose be as God's messenger?

Interpret

Compare the way God's character is described in these two passages. What do you notice that is the same about how God has acted in the past (Neh. 9) and what Malachi says God will do on the Day of the Lord?

It can be difficult to read about God's judgment. Still, can you think of any reason why it might be *good news* that God takes sin so seriously?

Apply

How does thinking about God's loyalty to his people encourage you in your own walk with him? If you feel comfortable, share where in your life you most need his healing and mercy (Mal. 4:2).

Connecting the Bible's Big Story

Read Matthew 3:1–12. How does Matthew draw on Malachi's prophecy (as well as Isaiah's in Isa. 40:3) about a messenger who would prepare the way for the Messiah?

Read Luke 24:13–27. We read this passage together in Week 1 of this study. How do these verses help us understand the big story we see unfolding throughout the Bible?

 Gospel Application

When God's people hear his law read to them in Nehemiah 8, they bow with their faces to the ground and weep. Confronted with their rebellion against God and his covenant, they grieve the ways they have dishonored him. This historical event reminds us how crucial it is to hear God's Word and to let it shape our lives, just as we have tried to do together throughout this study.

But as God's people rebuild the walls of Jerusalem and renew their covenant relationship with God, they are still in need of a Savior. At the end of the Old Testament, they are waiting for the prophet like Elijah that Malachi promises will come before the Messiah. They will have to wait for 400 years, just as God's people waited 400 years for their rescue from Egypt.

God's covenant promises start coming true in the story of the New Testament. An angel appears to an elderly couple in Jerusalem named Zechariah and Elizabeth, announcing that they will have a son. He will serve in the spirit and power of Elijah, preparing the way for God to return and dwell with his people.

When Jesus finally arrives, he fulfills every promise God has ever made. He comes in human form, dwelling among us so that he can offer his perfect life in our place. When he pours out his life on the cross, he bears the wrath we each deserve. And when he rises again, he conquers death so that we can live with him, now and forevermore. The story of the Old Testament makes us long for this Savior. The whole Bible points to Jesus—who lived, died, and rose again so that our God could dwell with his people forever.

Here is the good news of the Bible: *Our hope of being with God forever is not ultimately up to you and me.* Instead, it is on the basis of the life, death, and resurrection of Jesus, who came to rescue us.

So, when you have sinned, or when you wonder about God's presence and work in the world, read his Word. Turn from sin, and then give thanks for the loyal love of the God who gave his own Son *for you.*

Additional Bible Readings

Nehemiah 1; Malachi 3

Review Old Testament Timeline and Maps

Review the Temple section on the timeline.

Review the seventh map, *The Persian Empire.* Notice that Nehemiah works for Artaxerxes in Susa, before traveling to Jerusalem to rebuild the walls.

Dig Deeper with the *Old Testament Study Guide*

Read the last section of chapter nine: Temple (pp. 263-274).

Bible Study Notes

Invitation

Here we are, at the end of our great adventure through the Old Testament. I'm cheering you on for wrestling with some of the trickiest passages and themes in the Bible, and I pray that God has strengthened your heart and mind as he has met you in his Word.

Throughout our study, we have seen that God offers salvation to the very people who have sinned against him. He gives his own Son to redeem people who were far away, bringing them near to him. If you have never trusted in Jesus for salvation, I invite you to do so, using the prayer below as a guide.

God of all creation, you are the one true God and the author of history. Thank you for your Word, the Bible, which reveals who you are. I know that I have sinned against you, and I confess the ways I have put other things before you in my life. I am unable to fix myself or change my own heart—but I know that you can. I am putting my faith in Jesus, who lived the perfect life I have failed to live. Thank you for sending him to die in my place, taking my sin upon his shoulders to the cross, rising again from the dead. I believe that you now give me his righteousness so that I can have life with you now and forever. Please give me your Holy Spirit to walk with me and make me more like Jesus, even as I continue to wrestle with sin. And use my life however you choose to bring you glory in the world. Help me to love and follow Jesus, my King, until the day he comes again to make all things new. Amen.

If you have prayed this prayer, or you would like to know more about what it means to follow Jesus, please talk with a Christian parent, a local church pastor, or a youth leader. Any of these adults will be so excited to share with you and celebrate your steps of faith in Christ. Followers of Jesus are not meant to walk alone—God brings us into his faith family so that we can help and encourage each other in Christ.

I pray that this journey through the Old Testament has revealed more of God's great love for you. I encourage you to keep reading the Bible, always looking for Jesus at the center of the story. And I pray you will grow in his grace until he returns.

Chelsea Erickson

www.ingramcontent.com/pod-product-compliance
Lightning Source LLC
LaVergne TN
LVHW010840120826
845149LV00017B/3335
* 9 7 9 8 9 9 1 5 6 1 1 1 2 *